The Hidden Secret of the Apocalypse

The Hidden Secret of the Apocalypse

St. John's Revelation Decoded

Elizabeth MacDonald Burrows

SEABOARD PRESS

AN IMPRINT OF J. A. ROCK & CO., PUBLISHERS

The Hidden Secret of the Apocalypse: St. John's Revelation Decoded
by Elizabeth MacDonald Burrows

SEABOARD PRESS

is an imprint of James A. Rock & Company, Publishers

Address comments and inquiries to:
SEABOARD PRESS
900 South Irby Street, #508
Florence, South Carolina 29501
E-mail:
jrock@rockpublishing.com   lrock@rockpublishing.com
Internet URL: www.rockpublishing.com

Trade Paperback
ISBN-13/EAN: 978-1-59663-725-2

Library of Congress Control Number: 2008934465

Printed in the United States of America

First Edition: 2009

In Memory

of

John the Beloved

The man

who has

tantalized

the world

for

two thousand years

My Deep Appreciation to the Many Who Have
Helped to Make this Book Possible

Especially
Santosh Kumar Boddikuri

And

Miss Janet Berglund
Dr. Mary-Helene Brown
Mr. & Mrs. Chris Bundschu
Dr. & Mrs. Dennis Dossett
Miss Suzanne Gehrels
Rev. & Mrs. Benjamin Godair
Mr. Peter Hiatt
Mr. Tore Kvalvik
Miss Sandra Lundstrom
Miss Lorna Macdonald
Miss Rene Maurer
Mrs. Carolyn Meyer
Mrs. Karel Mottley
Dr. Nancy Potts
Dr. and Mrs. Ralph Sand
Mr. and Mrs. Ralph Sand III
Mr. Michael Shemett
Suzanne Smith, Esq.
Miss Cheryl Watkins
LTC and Mrs. Neil Weber

Contents

Introduction

*S*t. John's Revelation has existed in the misty corridors of time for 2,000 years, and its beasts and dragons have taxed the imagination of the human world just as long. It was not the only apocalypse to have been written by a disciple, for Paul and Thomas both tried their hand at monsters and Satan's burning torment. It was St. John's work, however, which struck the fancy of the Nicene Council and they who selected it to take its place in the chronological records of holy dispensation. Surprisingly, it would not remain there long because the Council soon removed it, and, later, for whatever reason, they chose to include it again

Obviously, at the time of this apocalyptic controversy, the Council little realized that the text contained Christendom's most guarded secret, or they would have taken elaborate precautions to protect the sacred document from the eyes of the world. Since the final inclusion of John's Revelation, thousands of writers and scholars have entered the bottomless pit of the apocalypse to fight its mighty earthquakes and brimstone, but few have risen victorious from its fiery inferno. Twenty centuries have passed and still the multi-headed dragon rules over the dark shadows of ignorance and superstition, challenging anyone who dares enter into the apocalyptic abyss.

The primary question concerning the mystery of the Revelation, which is clearly one of the most misunderstood writings of all time, is why is this work so complex? One answer is obvious; the writing is primarily allegorical. The second reason is more obscure, for it relates to the spiritual transformation of human to divine, known as the *Resurrection of the Dead*, the most hidden secret of the early church. Although the *Resurrection*, under such names as *Soul Consciousness, Transformation of Human to Divine,*

Baptism of the Holy Spirit, Messianic Initiation, and last, but not least, *Crucifixion of the Soul,* has been the central focus of philosophical and religious studies for over six thousand years it has primarily been taught in secret and passed only from master to disciple. Therefore the early Bishops felt licensed to preserve the sacred rites which would change the course of human reasoning, for they felt they had been directly consecrated by the followers of Christ. As the centuries passed, this exalted prophecy of human destiny became relegated to ritualistic practices, and its mysteries ultimately lost to a world which believes itself to be more mortal than immortal.

Evidence of the great secrecy surrounding the secret teachings of Christianity is found in the writings of St. Dionysius, Clemons, and Tertullian. St. Dionysius, first Bishop of Athens, once stated that the tradition of the sacrament is said to be divided into three Degrees, or grades, which are purification, initiation, and accomplishment, or perfection.

The *Apostolic Constitutions*, attributed to Clemens, Bishop of Rome, describes the early church, saying, "These regulations must on no account be communicated to all sorts of persons, because of the Mysteries contained in them." It speaks of the Deacon's duty to keep the doors closed, thereby preventing any uninitiated from entering the oblation. The Ostiarii, or doorkeepers, kept guard, and gave notice of the time of prayer and church-assemblies. The Mysteries were said to be open to the Fidels or Faithful only; and no spectators were allowed at the communion.

Tertullian, who died about AD. 216, says in his *Apology:* "None are admitted to the religious Mysteries without an oath of secrecy. We appeal to your Tracian and Eleusian Mysteries, and we are especially bound to this caution, because if we prove faithless, we should not only provoke Heaven, but draw upon our heads the utmost rigor of human displeasure. And should strangers betray us? They know nothing but by report and hearsay. Far hence, ye profane! is the prohibition from all holy Mysteries."

Clemons, Bishop of Alexandria, born about AD. 191, said, in his *Stromata,* that he could not explain the Mysteries because he should thereby, according to the old proverb, put a sword into the hands of a child.

Archelaus, Bishop of Cascara in Mesopotamia, says: "These Mysteries the Church now communicates to him who has passed through the introductory Degree. They are not explained to the Gentiles at all; nor are they taught openly in the hearing Catechumens: but much that is spoken is in disguised terms, that the Faithful, who possess the knowledge, may be still more informed, and those who are not acquainted with it may suffer no disadvantage."

St. Gregory Nazianzen, Bishop of Constantinople, AD. 379, states: "You have heard as much of the Mystery as we are allowed to speak openly in the ears of all; the rest will be communicated to you in private and that information you must retain within yourself … .Our Mysteries are not to be made known to strangers."

In view of overwhelming evidence of the Church's early secrecy, it has gradually become obvious to people in the modern world that there were, and are, actually two teachings of the scriptures. One of these teachings is literal, or outer, and the other is hidden, or inward. Not only is the evidence of secrecy a factor in determining this, but there are two other another primary causes. One: Twentieth century technology is daily tearing asunder the myths and ideology of the past in the fields of evolution and creation. Two: The rapid advancement of the human mind.

The advancing mental process of the human race, having journeyed through matter in the corporeal form and built vast empires in the fields of science, religion, and philosophy, is no longer relegated to ideas and concepts of the past. Instead, humanity has started an insistent search into the meaning of life. People 2,000 years ago might have believed in beasts and dragons as portrayed in St. John's Revelation, but modern science and archaeology can prove that such creatures did not exist then, do not exist now, and will not exist in the future. To a world which has landed on the moon, soared into outer space, and reached into the past to ten to the minus forty three seconds, a fraction of a second after the universe began; the shackles of mythology are forced to release their mighty chains. The dogmas of the past are dying, and that is as it should be. A new world can only rise above the rubble of the old if it releases itself from the bondage of yesterday's limitation, and this includes the analysis of St. John's Revelation.

The search for new inroads into the apocalypse can be very difficult and confusing, primarily because of the complex symbolism. First, the scholar must have a true understanding of creation as it is found in the original Hebrew Genesis. This means that it is essential to turn to such books as the *Hebraic Tongue Restored* by Fabre d' Olivet, because those who seek to utilize any of the more traditional text are sure to find a tree blocking their path. An example of such an obstacle can best be understood by a scriptural comparison between the King James version of the Holy Bible and original Hebrew, Moses' native tongue.

King James, Gen.2:2, states, "And on the seventh day God ended his work which he had made; and rested on the seventh day from all his work which he had made."

The Cosmogony of Moses (original Hebrew), Genesis 2:2, however, states: "And-he-fulfilled, He-the-Gods, in-the light's manifestation-the-seventh, the sovereign-work which-he-had-performed; and-he-restored-himself, in-the-light's manifestation the-seventh, from-the-whole-sovereign work-which-he-had-performed."

Interpretation of St. James version leads one to believe that there will be no further progress for the human species, and that human beings are relegated forever to the sixth phase, or sixth day of creation. Thus, the human race can never become any thing more than they already are. Also, one might tend to believe in a God who sits on a throne somewhere in the sky and who took a nap after He created man and woman. None of this is true, of course, as evidenced by scientific, philosophical, and religious evolution. Neither can St. John's Revelation be interpreted on this basis.

The Cosmogony of Moses from original Hebrew infers that another phase of human evolution lies ahead in which the Light of God will be resurrected in every living soul. In other words, heaven will become manifest on earth (descent of the new Israel), through the birth of God in mankind. Having restored this true meaning of the seventh day, or seventh epoch of Creation, it is easy to see that the Apocalypse actually refers to the transformation of human to divine, and that the royal battle (Armageddon) is not an outer war, but a battle which takes place between these two natures living within every corporeal being.

Next, it is necessary to decode the symbolism of the Tabernacle in the Wilderness. While this may not seem necessary at first, it is essential, as much of the apocalyptic symbolism relating to metals, colors and stones, originates there. If the Tabernacle is analyzed according to the original, or hidden, teachings of Moses, then its three compartments pertain to: (1) the outer court - the body, (2) the room of the Holy - the soul, and (3) the room of the Holy of the Holies containing the Ark of the Covenant -the Spirit. The Ark of the Covenant contained in the room of the Holy of the Holies therefore signifies the divine spark of God existing in the spiritual nature of the soul. To open or pierce the Ark, necessitates that the soul must release itself from its fascination of human life and journey inward toward its spiritual counterpart, (the apocalyptic indwelling Christ), in order to come unto the throne of God containing the *Law* which will govern the soul thereafter.

This is clearly revealed through the clues left in the room of the Holy (soul). The twelve loaves of shewbread are arranged in two stacks of six, thereby signifying the two natures (soul and its indwelling Divine Nature) bound to the worldly matter (sixth day, or the sixth epoch). These two must become one (1-2, or 12) in order to accomplish the last days, or final phase of human progression in which the indwelling Christ reins supreme over the worldly ways of humanity.

Similarity between the symbolism of Moses and John does not end here but goes even further, for the colors, as well as the metals used in the Tabernacle in the Wilderness play a very important role. Base metals such as brass and bronze represent the base, or lesser nature of a human being, even as silver signifies the soul, and gold, the incumbent spirit of the indwelling God, or the indwelling Christ. For instance, Revelation 1:12-15 reads as follows:

Rev. 1:12: And I turned to see the voice that spake with me. And being turned, I saw seven gold candlesticks;

Rev. 1:13: And in the midst of the seven candlesticks one like unto the son of man, clothed with a garment down to the foot, and girt about the paps with a golden girdle.

Rev. 1:14: His Head and his hairs were white like wool, as white as snow; and his eyes were as a flame of fire;

Rev. 1:15: And his feet like unto fine brass, as if they burned in a furnace: and his voice as the sound of many waters.

If these scriptures are interpreted according to the mysteries pertaining to the *Resurrection of the Dead*, they reveal the transformation of human nature into its divine heritage in the following manner:

On the seventh day (epoch) of creation (seven gold candlesticks, each signifying a single epoch of earth's evolution—according to Genesis) there rose one like unto the Son of man (born of woman's body; Son of God denotes one who has passed through the resurrection by raising the indwelling Christ who is the Son of God). Although his mystery was not fully revealed (clothed to the feet symbolizes that the main body of the mystery is hidden), he came forth wearing a golden girdle, or bearing the wisdom of God (gold)[1]

His hair was white to represent the purification of the soul (wool is carded and cleaned in order to be spun into thread, while snow signifies winter, or dying. In this case dying of the corporeal ways), and his eyes of flame (fire burns and purifies) pierced all which was hidden. That which had been impure lived no more (brass-base, or a mortal nature which had been burned and purified), and his voice was in many languages (waters).

Summary; one can safely reason that John is saying that the divine nature, or indwelling Christ, will come forth to lead every living soul into the seventh, or final evolutionary phase of creation, through wisdom and purification.

Lastly, the scholar must have some knowledge of the Essenes, particularly in deciphering the angels of the Apocalypse. The Essenes kept their angelology a secret and the most profound mysteries of Revelation would have remained just that if it were not for Professor Edmond S. Bordeaux, philologist, and former professor at the University of Cluj. During his studies in the Archives of the Roman Vatican, Professor discovered that the teachings of the Essenes were an integral part of the secret teachings of Jesus the Christ. This not only settled the question once and for all as to whether Jesus ever studied with the Essenes, but also linked John the Beloved to this mysterious sect. According to the Vatican manuscript, "*The Lost Jesus Scroll*," it was John who recorded Jesus' teachings regarding the utilization of natural and cosmic law which governs the universe.

In the *Lost Jesus Scroll* Jesus taught the process by which the resurrection could be accomplished, saying;

The Holy Temple can be built only with the ancient communions, those which are spoken, those which are thought, and those which are lived. For if they are spoken only with the mouth, they are as a dead hive which the bees have forsaken, and that gives no more honey.

*"The communions are a bridge between man and the
angels, and like bridge, can be built only with patience,
yea, even as a bridge over the river is fashioned stone by
stone, as they are found in the water's edge.*

*And the communions are fourteen in number, as the
angels of the Heavenly Father number seven, and the angels
of the Earthly Mother number seven.*

There no longer remains any doubt that the disciples who
traveled with Jesus when he lived on earth were initiated into certain secret teachings, particularly those pertaining to *raising of the
dead.* Some went on to achieve this sanctified state, among these,
St. John the Beloved.

Those who walked with the Master, however, were not the
only ones to enter the holy metamorphosis. Others people discovered the key to the mysteries, such as St. Benedict, St. Jerome,
St. Francis of Assisi, St. John of the Cross, and St. Theresa of
Avila. These do not walk alone, for since the formation of the
early Church the list of the names of those who have passed through
the transformation of human to divine (*Resurrection of the Dead*)
has grown. The powerful message now encompassing the third
planet from the earth's sun has begun to change its focus from
"being saved" to *"the resurrection."*

In many instances the Church turned against the great Christian mystics, referring to them and their work as heretic. Today
fundamental rigidity is losing this hold, for darkness and unknowing has never been able to stamp out the light and wisdom of
idealistic precepts. Time and again truth has stirred the branches
of the Tree of Life and threatened the old beliefs with the icy kiss
of death. Just as often, the Church has raised its sword of subjuga-
tion to fight the encroaching and foreboding shadow of change.
Usually it has risen victorious, but each time a few dedicated people
have turned away from conventional practices to travel the difficult less obvious road of enlightenment and wisdom. These few

have managed to leave their mark ingrained in the rivers of spirituality which flow through an ever changing earth. The powerful and ever-expanding intellect of the human race can not be halted; it will move across the earth's surface like a mighty wind, leaving a new edifice behind dedicated to the peaceful co-existence of the human family and the descent of a new Israel.

The Church deserves some defense, however, for after the early years of secrecy it did not necessarily intend to withhold information from the people. It is a fact, that those who governed the growth of Christendom no longer understood the deeper and inner mysteries, because the teachings had long been cloaked in secrecy and bound by ritualistic practices. The religious writings, including the *official* cannon of the Bible, have been translated, revised and modified, so many times by intellectual, but not necessarily illumined, scholars, that the great foundation of Christianity ultimately became lost in a literal application common to the masses. That which could not be understood was placed under wraps of obscurity and denounced as non biblical or heretical texts. By the twentieth century, widespread education of the masses sparked an intellectual revolution. Knowledge was no longer relegated to a gift of the Holy Spirit, or to the small percentage of humans who could read and write, but rose in shrouded splendor to encompass the whole human race through a new word called academia.

A new epoch is now dawning, and with it the Light of the Apocalypse will burst forth upon the world like a titanic sun, although some theologians and scholars may not agree. It is also possible that they will not wish to agree with the interpretation presented forthwith because the apocalypse shall not appear as prophecy of doom and destruction, but rather a prophecy of sublime hope. And the seven days of creation shall not remain seven week days, but seven epochs of earth changes covering billions of years.

In view of his disclosures in the *Lost Jesus Scroll, Gospel of John, Acts of John,* and *John's Revelation,* John can no longer remain a simple martyr. By completing the process of the resurrection and achieving the unitive state between the soul and the indwelling Christ, he has stepped into the arena of the elect who have pierced the web of darkness and unknowing to live and breathe in another world not bound by the fetters of corporeal limitations. Such realization sheds new light on John's life, and Patmos no longer signifies a place of exile and imprisonment, but a place of exalted transformation. His quiet sojourn on the island enabled him to form his *Apocalypse*, not only as he experienced it, but as the collective world consciousness would experience it some day.

Unfortunately John's *Revelation* is extraordinarily complex and one can only wonder how, and why, it has survived for two thousand years. Perhaps it is because it holds a subtle promise of a new world and whispers a mighty secret in the sands of time, a secret of transformation and redemption for a struggling humanity. If so, it has kept its secret well, for even today it still stands in shrouded splendor to challenge and baffle theologians and scholars of all faiths.

Before entering the main text of St. John's Revelation, it is better to have some understanding of its basic concept. One must begin with the fact that every terrestrial being is comprised of three parts: the body, or temporal housing which enables the soul to function on earth; the soul which has been created in the image of God, but drawn deeply into matter by its attraction to worldly things; and finally the indwelling Christ, the divine nature whose foundation is in heaven. This guardian of the soul, however, is inhibited to some degree by the soul's attraction to the world of matter. For most part the soul feels itself to be human as opposed to divine, because it has been entranced by the dance of human life and seeks its fulfillment through multifarious adventures.

One day, the soul begins its search for a deeper meaning to life and a need to know God. Soon the pangs of new birth stirs within it like a gentle breeze flowing through the verdant leaves of a mighty forest. During this period, the indwelling Christ begins his courtship of the soul, eventually drawing it away from its earthly attachments in preparation for their holy union. Since the Christ is a divine aspect of God and thereby endowed with all powers, it is his pre-assigned responsibility to purify the soul and draw it into oneness with him. It is only through this holy union that the soul reaches oneness with God and exchanges mortality for immortality.

This exalted transfiguration of the soul from human to divine is symbolized in the Apocalypse by countless numbers. Among such numbers are the 12,000 - the soul and the indwelling Christ (2) must be merged into one (1) through the union of the body, soul and spirit (000), and 1,000, the union or oneness, of the body, soul and spirit with its divine counterpart.. The 144,000 refers to the indwelling Christ, who is bound to the world of senses by the nature of four major elements which formed the earth (4) and, the soul which is also bound to the world of matter by nature of these same four elements, (4-4). These two parts must become one (1) through the union of the body, soul, and spirit (000). In surrender to this union the soul is brought into the state of immortality (at-one). This heralds its entry into the seventh and final phase of human progression (seventh epoch), for the soul has mastered the temptations of corporeality, or 666 the sign of the beast; bondage of the body, soul, and spirit to the sixth day of progression, or sixth epoch, known as human life. See Genesis 1:26 through 1:31.

Although the foregoing represents only an infinitesimal part of St. John's *Revelation,* it is nonetheless the basic foundation of the entire text, and applies to everything from beasts and dragons to angels. The numerous anthropos (composite figures representing either the lesser or corporeal nature of human life, or the celestial forces which serve the indwelling Christ) also further complicate the giant puzzle. Therefore it becomes necessary to dissect every aspect of the strange creatures which rambles through the corridors of the apocalyptic maze, and dissection is certainly the key. None of the anthropos can be interpreted as a whole creature. It would be rather tautological to go more deeply into the mysteries pertaining to the skeletal remains of St. John's anthropos at this time, however, for each is addressed individually as the Apocalypse unfolds.

The inextricability of the apocalyptic mysteries produces yet one final task, and that is to present St. John's Revelation to the world in a comprehensive, but interesting form. In some ways this is almost as difficult as interpreting it, for to break down every single symbol into lengthy explanations and multitudinous footnotes would produce a book so massive that only an occasional scholar would condescend to read it. Revelation is beautiful and holds such an inspiring promise, however, long drawn out procedures will simply not do it justice.

At first glance it will appear that everything has been changed in the scriptural interpretation of the Odyssey, and in some ways it has, but only to the extent that every scripture now appears in its true meaning rather than shrouded in symbolism. Since no piece of the puzzle will remain concealed and all of the pieces will fit perfectly, and because the conclusions are logical as evidenced through the systematic progression of natural law, there should be little doubt as to its accuracy. A summary is included at the beginning of each chapter, thereby reducing the cyclopean number of footnotes required. To further simplify the presentation of the work, the new apocalyptic scripture will appear on the left and the King James Version on the right. This will provide a constant means of comparison and eliminate the inconvenience of switching from one book to another.

Rev. 21:7

He that overcometh shall inherit all things;
And I will be his God, and he shall be my son.

SECTION I

TITLE

The Royal Battle

CHAPTER I

Glory of Revelation

*Jesus said to them: When you make the two one, and when
you make the inner as the outer and the outer as the inner
and the above as the below, and when you make the male
and the female into a single one, so that the male will
not be male and the female not be female,
then you shall enter the Kingdom.*

Gospel of Thomas
Log. 22:24

As the curtain rises on the mighty drama which will be enacted within the following pages, the eyes behold a hidden passageway leading into the dark unknown caverns of war, mystery, and intrigue. By this time the soul has become entranced by her divine counterpart, the indwelling Christ; feminine pronoun is used here because the soul is always approached as the bride of the Lamb, whether it is in a male or female embodiment. He has led the soul to the brink of a terrible abyss known as the *dark night.* Suddenly, without warning, the soul is plunged into the very depths of apocalyptic storms, tidal waves, beasts, and dragons. Swirling through the intangible mists of transformation, the soul soon finds its self in the center of a colossal battle arena surrounded by two great armies, each one armed with terrible weapons of war. On one side, the warriors of indiscretion and desires and on the other side a great white knight with his legion of angels.

The drama of the Apocalypse begins as John speaks of his imprisonment on Patmos, one of the small islands belonging to a group called *Sporades* located in the Aegean sea. He states that he is in Spirit, a state of consciousness linking the finite mind with the infinite mind of God, and through this heightened awareness he is experiencing the future transfiguration of earth. It is also the Lord's Day, signifying that he had been raised from the bondage of human fascination and had entered into the seventh or final epoch of human progression in which divine man is born from the ashes of human suffering.

In the opening scriptures John is shown the things which are to come to pass. The apocalyptic battle between human and divine begins with seven angels who stand around the throne of God. These are the same seven angels who will pour their vials of woe on the corporeal nature in the last hours of the mighty war, after which mankind finally surrenders to Divine will, thereby ending the reign of human rulership.

John the Beloved is not using the words *Jesus Christ* in the light of a human/divine personage, but is referring to the Spirit, the indwelling Christ, or the divine aspect of God incarnate in every living being.. This is difficult for many to understand because of the complexities in separating Jesus Christ, the Master and the man, from the terms Savior and anointed, the knighted champion of the soul. If this task of separation is not accomplished, however, the mystery of the apocalypse remains within locked corridors of unanswerable parable.

At the beginning of the narrative, the apostle turns to see who is speaking to him and sees one like unto the son of man. He warns the churches of Asia Minor that this divine presence will come forth with clouds (not revealed) and that every eye will see him, as well as those who have pierced the mystery of him: and that all kindreds of the earth will wail because of him. This last segment of the preceding statement appears somewhat strange at first, particularly since the world has breathlessly awaited the fulfillment of the apocalyptic prophecy and the appearance of a divine savior who would herald the final days of human existence. Can it be possible that the fulfillment of prophecy also brings forth some terrible reprisal which only an elect few can escape, or is it perhaps some mysterious innuendo and parable? The answer to this will be revealed as the Apocalypse unfolds, for to approach such a glorious exodus without proper foundation would lessen its impact.

In Rev. 1: 8, a divine apparition has appeared to John and speaks, saying that He is Alpha and Omega, the beginning and the end, which is, which was, and which is yet to come. This statement can only be interpreted properly through the light of Moses' Cosmogony, for in the beginning, Light came out of darkness. This does not refer to the light of a sun, but the manifestation of the first principle of God from whence all creation originated (Gen:1:3). Therefore, this divine presence of prophecy can represent none other than that Light which came forth in the beginning, which lives in all creation, but which does not completely rule over the soul because of its affinity to matter. He indicates, however, that he is yet to come.

A major key to unraveling the secret of the *last days* is carefully hidden in these words, for they indicate that He, the indwelling Christ, will be brought forth in all mankind and that He will rule in the end.

In Rev. 1:13, John describes this divine presence as one like unto the son of man, meaning human born from woman's womb. (Son of God depicts one who has resurrected the indwelling Light, or raised the dead.) In that he is clothed from his head to his feet, he personifies the apocalyptic mysteries not yet revealed. The process by which this is to be accomplished is found in the symbolism of His attire, for he is girded with a golden girdle to denote wisdom (gold-wisdom, silver-soul, brass, or copper, - base nature see: Exodus 35 through 39). His feet were as fine brass, to signify that his corporeal nature has been purified by fire. In this instance, and in all apocalyptic traditions forthcoming, fire represents purification, after the manner of sacrificial offerings.

In the sacrificial rites of Moses, it was customary for an animal to be offered to the fires of cremation in order that the flesh, or material nature be destroyed. This would enable the soul to free itself from its fleshy counterpart and rise new born to God. Therefore Rev. 1:7-13 might best be summed up in the following manner:

In the final days of human embodiment, the Light (indwelling Christ) will be raised within every soul and reveal all errors of human judgment. In turn, the indiscretions of the soul will be purified by the Light after the manner of an animal which has been offered to the fires of cremation.

As the Apocalypse continues, John further describes this beguiling figure of redemption who has come to him, as standing in the midst of seven angels, representing the seven epochs the soul must complete (seven gold candlesticks). He is holding seven stars in his right hand, the seven purifying forces of Divine will.

This segment of the text would be difficult to reiterate without some knowledge of Essene angelology, for these fourteen angels, according to Mosaic and Essene traditions, are actually the fourteen forces of Natural and Cosmic Law emanating from God which established creation. These are represented in both the seven prong candlestick and the Essene Tree of Life. In their proper sequence the fourteen forces, comprised of the seven laws of nature and the seven laws of Divine will, reveal the systematic process by which earth was formed, by which it progresses, and by which it will end.

It can be said, therefore, that power brought forth the sun, while the cohesive force of love was, and is, the cause of unity and reproduction. The wisdom of God's Divine Plan caused, and causes, the systematic forward thrust of progression, in turn forcing the hot molten planets to move into cold unmanifested space. This systematic motion produced air, while the unity between fire and space brought forth mighty rains. Eventually, life began to develop from midst the throes of orderly process, life which was subject to constant change but eternal in its constitutional makeup. Eventually, through creative work, life began to domesticate the earth upon which it lived. It ate of the fruit of the vines for the health of its body, and in time it matured its reasoning and began the long search for both peace and joy. However, it found it could not have joy without peace.

At the end of the sixth day of creation, or sixth epoch, which brought forth the human species, the soul turns toward the heavens to learn the reasons for its suffering, old age, and death. Perceiving the indwelling Light it brings forth this Light, entreating the Spirit of God to descend upon Earth (descent of the Spirit to live in the flesh) thereby establishing the final evolutionary cycle of human life, or the descent of the New Jerusalem. This transformation would constitute the end of the known world.

In the traditional and elegant style which will become so familiar as the Apocalypse progresses, St. John closes the first chapter by saying that when he saw the powerful emissary of God who held the seven stars and possessed the two-edged sword (truth and justice) he fell at his feet as dead. However, the holy emissary reaches out with his right hand (right hand signifies righteousness) and touches him, saying,; *Fear not; I am the first and the last: I am he that liveth and was dead: and, behold, I am alive for evermore, Amen: and have the keys of hell and of death.*"

As the curtain descends on the first chapter, the somber but beautiful closing words of God's divine ambassador indicate that he is the Light, the indwelling Christ, which was brought forth in the beginning, but became as dead by his descent to journey with the soul through matter. Now he has been resurrected and will live forever, although he holds the keys to heaven and hell which is a subtle warning that he has come forth to temper the soul with truth and justice.

⮞⮜

1. God revealed His divine plan to Jesus Christ, the Master, so that Jesus could instruct his followers in those things which were shortly to occur. An angel was sent forth to John, who was on the Isle of Patmos.

1. The Revelation of Jesus Christ, which God gave unto him, to shew his servants things which must shortly come to pass; and he sent and signified it by his angel unto his servant John.

2. It was decreed that John should record all things which he saw.

2. Who bare record of the word of God, and of the testimony of Jesus Christ, and all things that he saw.

3. Those who receive the mysteries of the *Resurrection of the Dead* (raising the indwelling Christ) and live according to the criterion revealed by the Revelation will achieve immortality (cessation of darkness, unknowing and human death).

3. Blessed is he that readeth, and they that hear the words of this prophecy, and keep those things which are written therein; for the time is at hand.

4. John wrote to the seven churches, saying, "Grace to you and peace from God, which created all life and has existed since beginning, and His Spirit which is yet to be brought forth in all mankind; and from the seven Cosmic Laws (seven epochs which brought forth creation).

4. John to the seven churches which are in Asia: Grace be unto you, and peace, from him which is, and which was, and which is to come; and from the seven Spirits which are before the throne.

5. "And from the indwelling Christ, which has witnessed all things. He is the Light now raised from his imprisonment to matter (death and darkness) where the soul has bound him because of its sense attraction to earthly things. He loved us, and thereby descended (blood-sacrifice) into matter, assuring the soul of a resurrection.[1]

5. And from Jesus Christ, who is the faithful witness, and the first begotten of the dead, and the prince of the kings of earth. Unto him that loved us, and washed us from our sins in his own blood.

6. "And by abiding in us, has made us kings and priests before God, his Father; May he be glorified and have dominion forever and ever.

6. And hath made us kings and priests unto God and his father; to him be glory and dominion for ever and ever. Amen

7. "Behold, he comes from that which is hidden (clouds) and every eye shall see him, and they also who opened the door to the mysteries of the resurrection (pierced the nature of the immortality of the soul). And all people of earth shall grieve over their violations against the way of heaven because of him.[2]

7. Behold, he cometh with clouds; and every eye shall see him, and they also which pierced him: and all kindreds of the earth shall wail because of him. Even so, Amen.

8. "I am the beginning and the end, for I am now, I have always been, and will be that which is yet to come, for I am the eternal."

8. I am Alpha and Omega, the beginning and the ending, saith the Lord, which is, and which was, and which is yet come, the Almighty.

9. I, John, am your brother and companion, and have entered into the tribulation of the *Resurrection.* I ascended into this state of transformation under the indwelling Christ while on the Isle of Patmos—because I spoke the truth of God and testified to the Christ in Jesus.

9. I, John, who also am your brother, and companion in tribulation, and in the kingdom and patience of Jesus Christ, was in the isle that is called Patmos, for the word of God, and for the testimony of Jesus Christ.

10. I was one in God (Spirit), having entered the seventh epoch and final phase of human progression, and I heard a great voice like a trumpet behind me.

10. I was in the Spirit on the Lord's Day, and heard behind me a great voice, as of a trumpet.

11. Saying: "I am he who was in the beginning and I am the last to come forth on earth. You must write these things which I show you in a book, and send it to the seven churches in Asia.

11. Saying, I am Alpha and Omega, the first and last: and, what thou seest, write in a book and send it unto the seven churches which are in Asia; unto Ephesus, and unto Smyrna, and Pergamos, and unto Thyatira, and unto Sardis, and unto Philadelphia, and unto Laodicea.

12. I turned to see the voice which spoke to me and I saw seven golden candlesticks (seven epochs of planetary progression).[3]

12. And I turned to see the voice that spake with me. And being turned, I saw seven golden candlesticks.

13. From the midst of the seven candlesticks, there came one of human countenance, as though born of woman. He revealed not his mystery for he was clothed (hidden) to the feet with a garment and girded with wisdom (golden girdle)

13. And in the midst of the seven candlesticks one like unto the Son of man, clothed with a garment down to the foot, and girt about the paps with a golden girdle.

14. His head and his hair were as white wool, symbolizing purity (white) and atonement (carded wool). His eyes, were as flames, for they would pierce the innermost secrets of the soul and destroy its adversities, as a fire destroys.

14. His head and his hairs were white like wool, as white as snow; and his eyes were as a flame of fire.

15. His feet were like fine brass (body-brass), signifying that he would purge the earthly nature of its impurities; His voice was the voice of many waters (all nations).

15. And his feet like unto fine brass, as if they burned in a furnace; and his voice as the sound of many waters.

16. In his right hand he controlled the seven cosmic forces[4] and out of his mouth went a two edge sword (truth and justice). His countenance shone as the power of the sun.[5]

16. And he had in his right hand seven stars: and out of his mouth went a sharp two-edged sword: and his countenance was as the sun shineth in his strength.

17. When I saw him I fell at his feet as dead. And he laid his right hand (divine benediction) on me, saying, "Fear not, for I am the first born in God and last to be raised in mankind."

17. And when I saw him, I fell at his feet as dead. And he laid his right hand upon me, saying unto me, Fear not; I am the first and the last:

18. I am he who has lived as Light from the beginning and I died in man through my descent to abide in him. Human fetters have imprisoned me since the world began. Behold I have now been *resurrected from the dead* and shall henceforth rule over the soul forever. I hold the key of hell (the impure regions of the soul known as the sub-conscious) and of death (darkness and unknowing).

18. I am he that liveth, and was dead; and, behold, I am alive for evermore. Amen; and have the keys of hell and death.

19. Write concerning these things which you have seen, the things which are, and those things which are yet to come upon all mankind.

19. Write the things which thou hast seen, and the things which are, and the things which shall be hereafter;

20. The mystery of the seven stars which you saw in my right hand are seven forces emanating from God. These signify the seven aspects of Cosmic Law which are represented by the seven churches[6]

20. The mystery of the seven stars which thou sawest in my right hand, and the seven golden candle-sticks. The seven stars are the angels of the seven churches: and the seven candle-sticks which thou sawest are the seven churches.

CHAPTER II

The Seven Churches

Not every one that saith unto me, Lord, Lord, shall enter
into the kingdom of heaven; but he that doeth the
will of my Father which is in heaven.

Matthew 7:21

The following chapter is full of complex symbolism, but it is also important to the interpretation of the Apocalypse. John is in an illumined, or ascended state of mind, as was Moses during his awakening on Sinai. As founder of the seven churches of Asia Minor, John is shown the weaknesses of each church. Yet, these same errors are also present in every human being because of direct violation to the ways of heaven, known as natural and cosmic law, even though performed in ignorance.

In Ephesus the church has left its first love, i.e., broken both Jesus' and Moses' commandment to love God (Mathew 22:36-38 & Exodus 20:2-3). Instead, the church, as does human kind, elected to follow the more temporal and worldly way of life. For this reason, the church is cautioned to return to God in all ways or it would fail to survive (removal of the candlestick) and fulfill its destiny. If, however, the church of Ephesus returned to the first commandment, it would become a partaker of the Tree of Life. This would be accomplished by developing harmony with both heaven and earth through proper utilization of natural and cosmic law (the fourteen forces equated to the Tree of Life).

To the church of Smyrna, the message is given that there were many in the congregation who claimed to follow the Law of Moses, but did not. These were people who could quote the scriptures, but were not prone to live their disciplined ways. There were also those who were struggling to teach and abide by Jesus' teachings. They were told that they would succeed in *Raising the Dead*, for the devil (mankind's lower nature) would be cast into prison (soul possession by the indwelling Christ) and be in tribulation (Armageddon) until they returned to the one God (1-0-state of unity). Those who succeeded would receive the crown of life (symbol of the illumined mind) and would not be hurt by the second death. The second death refers to the return to power and glory by the Christ in mankind. The first death occurred when he created the soul, dwelled therein, and descended into the darkness and unknowing of the soul as it journeyed through matter. In the second death, the indwelling Christ is raised from the dead and restored as ruler over the soul, which has long been governed by its sense attraction to matter.

To the church of Pergamos the message is given that their work was known, and that the people were trying to live the teachings of Christ in spite of great difficulty. Nonetheless, they had among them some who held the doctrine of Balaam (Numbers 22-23). This did not mean that the congregation worshipped Balaam, but there were those among the people who did not accept the new doctrine and were attempting to thwart it after the manner of the Old Testament prophet. Also there were some among them who upheld the decision of Nicolas, who defended Archelaus in front of Caesar, in the slaughter of 3,000 Jews.

Those in the church who had not been converted to the new religion are now asked to repent, as the old concepts would be destroyed by truth and justice. To those people who could overcome the false concepts, the secret, or hidden, teachings (manna-wisdom) would be given, and they would obtain the white Philosopher's stone of wisdom (knowledge of the purification of the soul).

Next, the indwelling Christ speaks to the church of Thyatira concerning their work saying that the people's latter works would be greater than their first. However, there were those who continued to follow the old customs which destroyed life, happiness and peace. To illustrate these impurities, the Old Testament prophetess, Jezebel is used to represent the uncleanness still remaining in the soul.

The next lines are probably among the most powerful and revealing words in the Apocalypse, for the indwelling and resurrected Christ states; when he has been raised from the dead in man, he will purge all impurities remaining in the soul and dispense judgment to everyone according to their work. This is quite different than the judgment beliefs held by early Christians, but certainly much more realistic. He further states that those who are not knowledgeable in the mysteries of the resurrection should receive no other burden, for the weight of human life was sufficient unto itself. On the other hand, those who overcame would become masters of wisdom in future ages, and would receive the morning star (the sign of dawn and birth of God in mankind).

The risen Christ further speaks, saying that his rule over the people would be as unyielding, powerful, and strong as iron, and that he would shatter the impure and false ideals like the vessels of a potter.

1. The indwelling Christ, having been raised, signifying the seventh and final epoch of soul progression, comes forth with the seven forces of cosmic law and asks John to write to the Church of Ephesus, saying;

1. Unto the angel of the church of Ephesus write; These things saith he that holdeth the seven stars in his right hand, who walketh in the midst of the seven golden candlesticks.

2. I know your works, your labor and your patience, and how you cannot condone those who do not walk in the ways of heaven: and how you have tested those who say they are followers of Jesus the Christ, but are not.

2. I know thy works, and thy labour, and thy patience, and how thou canst not bear them which are evil: and thou hast tried them which say they are apostles, and are not, and hast found them liars.

3. You have borne condemnation with patience because of truth, and have labored. Neither have you been defeated.

3. And hast borne, and hast patience, and for my name's sake hast laboured and, hast not fainted.

4. However, I have something against you because you have departed from the first commandment "to love the Lord thy God (Matthew 22:36-38)."

4. Nevertheless I have somewhat against thee, because thou hast left thy first love.

5. Remember this Law and return to the first commandment, or you shall fail to complete your journey through the seventh and final phase of human progression, and remain bound to the fetters of darkness and unknowing.

5. Remember therefore from whence thou are fallen, and repent, and do the first works; or else I will come unto thee quickly, and will remove thy candle stick out of his place, except thou repent.

6. I know you hate those who uphold the defense of Archelaus by Nicholas of Damascus. I am also opposed to the ways of the unjust.[1]

6. But this thou hast, that thou hatest the deeds of the Nicolaitanes, which I also hate.

7. To those who understand the mysteries of the resurrection, of which I speak, and abide in its ways, I shall make partakers of eternal life and they shall dwell in the paradise of God.

7. He that hath an ear, let him hear what the Spirit saith unto the churches; To him that overcometh will I give to eat of the tree of life, which is in the midst of the paradise of God.-

8. To the church of Smyrna write; He who is the Light and first born of God, who descended into matter and the last to be brought forth in the soul of mankind, is now resurrected. He speaks, saying:

8. And unto the angel of the church in Smyrna write; these things saith the first and the last, which was dead, and is alive.

9. I know your works, your trials and your poverty, but you are rich because you partake of those things which are eternal. I also know about those who claim to follow the laws of Moses and call themselves Jews, yet follow the path of destruction.

9. I know thy works, and tribulation, and poverty, (but thou art rich) and I know the blasphemy of them which say they are Jews, and are not, but are the synagogue of Satan.

10. Do not fear these things which you suffer, for that which is temporal and carnal in you shall be cast into the prison of purification. Because of this, your soul shall be made pure, but you shall have tribulation until you become one with God (1-0 days). Be faithful to my ways, and I will give you the eternal Light and illumined mind.[2]

10. Fear none of those things which thou shalt suffer: behold, the devil shall cast some of you into prison, that ye may be tried; and ye shall have tribulation ten days: be thou faithful unto death, and I will give thee the crown of life.

11. Those who understand these words and overcome their bondage to the natural world will not be hurt by the death of that which is lesser in them (born into corporeal—1st death. resurrecting from matter to become Divine—2nd death).

11. He that hath an ear let him hear what the Spirit saith unto the churches; He that overcometh shall not be hurt of the second death.

12. To the church of Pergamos write; He who holds the sword of truth and justice has spoken, saying;

12. And to the angel of the church in Pergamos write; These things saith he which hath the sharp sword with two edges;

13. I know your works and where you heart is, and even the seat of your corporeal nature. I know also that you hold fast to my name and have not denied my faith, even when Antipas,[3] was slain.

13. I know thy works, and where thou dwellest, even where Satan's seat is: and thou holdest fast my name, and hast not denied my faith, even in those days wherein Antipas was my faithful martyr, who was slain among you, where Satan dwelleth.

14. Yet, I have a few things against you. You have those among you who are not partakers of the laws of heaven and walk in the ways of destruction. This lays waste to the body, mind and soul after the manner Balaam,[4] who cast a stumbling block before the children of Israel and caused the youth to co-mingle with the Midianite women.

14. But I have a few things against thee, because thou hast there them that hold the doctrine Balaam, who taught Balac to cast a stumbling block before the children of Israel to eat things sacrificed unto idols, and to commit fornication.

15. You also have those among you who hold to the doctrine of the Nicolaitanes, an action which I deplore.

15. So has thou also them that hold the doctrine of the Nicolaitanes, which thing I hate.

16. Seek therefore the path of the good, or I will come quickly and fight against them with the sword of truth and justice.

16. Repent; or else I will come unto thee quickly and will fight against them with the sword in my mouth.

17. I will allow those who do not fear to live the path of righteousness, and, who overcome the errors of human ways, to become partakers of a hidden knowledge which will purify their minds as a stone is made white by the tides of the sea. These shall behold the mystery of the Philosophers' stone (ancient symbol that represents a soul which is purified through trans-formation,) of *wisdom*.

17. He that hath an ear, let him hear what the Spirit saith unto the churches; To him that overcometh will I give to eat of the hidden manna, and will give him a white stone, and in the stone a new name written, which no man knoweth saving he that receiveth it.

18. To the church of Thyatira write: These things said the Son of God (indwelling Christ), who has eyes to pierce and purify the innermost depths of the soul, and whose feet are as fine brass (brass-physical world) indicating that he will purify the soul's corporeal, or mortal, nature.

18. And unto the angel of the church in Thyatira write; These things saith the Son of God, who hath his eyes like unto a flame of fire, and his feet are like fine brass.

19. I know your works, and charity, and service, faith, and your patience. Even so, your labors in the end shall be greater than in the beginning, for you will then have conquered your corporeal nature.

19. I know thy works, and charity, and service, and faith, and thy patience, and thy works; and the last to be more than the first.

20. Notwithstanding, I have a few things against you, because your souls are not yet purified. You still remained enticed by the senses to the false ways of human life, just as those who once followed in the way of the prophetess Jezebel (representation of the senses).[5]

20. Notwithstanding I have a few things against thee, because thou sufferest that woman Jezebel, which calleth herself a prophetess, to teach and to seduce my servants to commit fornication, and to eat things sacrificed unto idols.

21. Although the desires of the flesh have had sufficient time to change, there are still those among you who have not heeded my will and remained subservient to the false enticements of matter.

21. And I gave her space to repent of her fornication; and she repented not.

22. Behold! I will allow those who have chosen the ways of the corporeal world to remain in the ways of human. These shall continue participating in acts of violence, hatred, anger, sorrow, and death—until they too repent and cast off that which is against the ways of heaven.

22. Behold, I will cast her into a bed, and them that commit adultery with her into great tribulation, except they repent of their deeds.

23. I therefore shall be resurrected within every soul and will kill the passions of self-will which leads down the path of destruction. It will come to pass that all people shall come unto me, for I am the indwelling guardian of the soul who sees all things. I shall give to each according to their works, good for good and reprisals for evil.

23. And I will kill her children with death; and all the churches shall know that I am he which searcheth the reins and hearts: and I will give unto every one of you according to your works.

24. But to you, and to the rest of Thyatira who do not understand the mysteries of the resurrection, and who have not known the depths of Satan (Individual ego and lower nature of mankind), I will put not further burden on you.

24. But unto you I say, and unto the rest in Thyatira, as many as have not this doctrine, and which have not known the depths of Satan, as they speak; I will put upon you none other burden.

25. But hold fast to those things which you do understand until I, the indwelling Christ, am resurrected in you.

25. But that which ye have already hold fast till I come.

26. Those who overcome the power of the ego (Satan) and keep my works until they have completed the *resurrection of the dead* will receive power to rule over nations.

26. And he that overcometh, and keepeth my works unto the end, to him will I give power over nations.

27. These shall be as a rod of iron, hard and strong, and they shall go forth in righteousness to fight against darkness and unknowing. Their power will purify all nations, for they will smite the ideals of the unjust, the unwise and the ignorant, as a potter shatters his unworthy vessels. This iron-will of God is same as that which I have received from my father, for he and I are one.

27. And he shall rule them with a rod of iron; and the vessels of a potter shall they be broken to shivers; even as I received of my father.

28. And I will lead him into a resurrection, which is like unto the dawning of the morning star, and he shall no more know death.

28. And I will give him the morning star.

29. He who can understand, let him hear what I say to the churches.

29. He that hath an ear, let him hear what the spirit saith unto the churches.

I am grateful, Heavenly Father, for thou has raised me to an
Eternal height and I walk in the wonders of the plain.
Thou gavest me guidance to reach Thine eternal company
From the depths of the earth.
Thou has purified my body to join the army of angels
Of earth and my spirit to reach the congregation of the
Heavenly angels.
Thou gavest man eternity to praise at dawn dusk
Thy works and wonders in joyful song.

Thanksgiving Psalm, Dead Sea Scrolls
VI iii, 19-36, Theodore Gaster

CHAPTER III

Key of David

He that findeth his life shall lose it: and he that
loseth his life for my sake shall find it.

Matthew 10:39

This chapter is comprised of perennial instructions to the churches, as well as revelations pertaining to the transformation of the individual. As in Chapter II, the primary steps are outlined which can initiate the actual resurrection (Raising of the Dead) of the indwelling Christ. The stage is then set for the battle of Armageddon, the war between the self-will and divine will.

A message is given to the church of Sardis that its members should be watchful, and repent over any direct violation of natural and cosmic law. It is held that no one actually knows the unequivocal moment when the indwelling Christ might appear. However, there were some in the church who were worthy to be cloaked in white, meaning that some had been initiated into the mysteries of the resurrection and were living according to divine will.

White has been the traditional garment of those inaugurated into the sublime secrets of transformation for over 6,000 years. It signifies purity, or purification of the soul, as well as the proper attire for the holy union (marriage) between the soul and the indwelling Christ, for only through this union can the soul become one with God. In that true disciples of the "path" have already received the descent of the Spirit into the flesh through the resurrection (the resurrected Christ descends to champion the soul) and linked with that which is immortal, they are considered to have reached eternal life, or written into the book of life. On the other hand, those who continue to walk in darkness and ignorance are referred to as the dead or those not yet awakened, i.e., those not yet written in the book of life.

As with the other churches there are some who are in opposition to such teachings. Nevertheless, the indwelling Christ states that even these will also come to worship him and that those who have passed into the *resurrection* will be guided through certain tribulations which will come upon the whole earth. Obviously those who walk the higher path of soul consciousness will not be affected by the surrounding adversities in the same way as those enmeshed in mortality are affected by destruction and starvation. Although the elect will not necessarily be freed from human embodiment immediately, they can live in the world, but not be bound by it.

To the church of Philadelphia the instruction is given; that those who hold the key of David,[1] and have opened the doorway of the mysteries cannot shut it, but those who refuse to open it cannot understand. For this reason, the resurrected Christ informs the church that the mysteries pertaining to the *raising of the dead* have been administered to them and they will not be forgotten.

Since the illumined, or Christed, mind is looked upon as crowned with Light and wisdom (crown is the halo, or nimbus, which appears around those who have received the descent of the Spirit), the church of Philadelphia is advised to hold fast to its knowledge, lest the corporeal ways of its members disinherit them from the crown and cut them off from that which is divine. Those who were able to overcome, however, are told that they will become the pillars, or the foundation, of a new world in which the kingdom of heaven descends upon earth. Furthermore, they would also be looked upon as Christed, meaning the anointed, or the bearers of the indwelling Christ.

After this, John writes to the church of Laodicea stating that the indwelling Christ will not minister to those who are neither cold nor hot. This statement, of course, refers to the precise law of cause and effect set in motion by the forward movement of God's divine plan, for those who were neither hot nor cold represent those who might read the scriptures but do not live them, and are therefore not worthy to receive the descent of the spirit into the flesh. The church is also told that those with material wealth are not actually rich, but are subject to poverty, mental disorders, diseased bodies, old age, sickness, ignorance and hatred.

In order to overcome these obstacles, the church of Laodicea is advised to seek spiritual wisdom (gold) and purify (fire) its base nature, in order that the soul may be dressed in white raiment and overcome the shame of its past misdeeds. The church is further instructed to tell its people that they must repent the errors of their ways and that those who do not will be rebuked and chastened. Furthermore when the transformation takes place within the soul, each individual will receive whatever action is necessary for purification, according to the precise law of cause and effect. Finally, the indwelling Christ stipulates that He alone guards the doorway between the two worlds (i.e., that which is mortal and that which is immortal) and if anyone knocks He will come unto him.

The foregoing is a particularly interesting phrase, primarily because it indicates that the Christ in mankind must not only be resurrected, but then again descend into the lesser world of human awareness in order to guide the soul and further the great work of regeneration. The church of Laodicea is now told that it will henceforth abide as one with the indwelling Christ, who is one with God.

1. Inform the head of the church of Sardis, that he who holds the powers over heaven and earth, knows your works and your teachings, but you have not yet raised the dead (the indwelling Christ).

1. And unto the angel of the church in Sardis write; These things saith he that hath the seven Spirits of God, and the seven stars; I know thy works, that thou hast a name that thou livest, and art dead.

2. Therefore, be watchful and strengthen those things which are true, for there are some among you who are prepared for the resurrection.

2. Be watchful and strengthen the things which remain, that are ready to die: for I have not found thy works perfect before God.

3. Hold fast to that which you have seen and heard, and repent; if you do not, I will come upon you as a thief, and you shall not know the hour of my coming.

3. Remember therefore how thou hast received and heard, and hold fast, and repent. If therefore thou shalt not watch, I will come on thee as a thief, and thou shalt not know what hour I will come upon thee.

4. Those who have prepared themselves, however, and have not violated their souls shall walk with me. These souls have been purified (dressed in white) as a bride prepared for her husband and they are worthy.

4. Thou hast a few names even in Sardis which have not defiled their garments; and they shall walk with me in white: for they are worthy.

5. Those who overcome shall find their souls washed by the white sands of purification and burned in the fire of Light. These shall be counted among the immortal and I who dwell in them shall make them one with God, and they shall live among the angels.

5. He that overcometh, the same shall be clothed in white raiment; and I will not blot out his name out of the book of life, but I will confess his name before my Father, and before his angels.

6. He who understands, let him hear what I say.

6. He that hath an ear, let him hear what the Spirit saith unto the churches.

7. Write to the church in Philadelphia and inform them that I speak the truth, that I am holy and hold the key of mastery (see introduction Chapter 3). Nor can any man close the path of awakening which I have opened, or open the gateway of any soul which I have locked.

7. And to the angel of the church in Philadelphia write; These things saith he that is holy, he that is true, he that hath the key of David, he that openeth, and no man shutteth; and shutteth, and no man may openeth.

8. I know your works and I have set before you an open door leading to the Kingdom of Heaven which cannot be closed by any mortal. You have shown some strength, and you have abided by my teachings and not denied my name.

8. I know thy works: behold, I have set before thee an open door, and no man can shut it: for thou has a little strength, and hast kept my word, and hast not denied my name.

9. Beware of those who yet belong to the synagogue of Satan (bound by the mortal nature) and have not passed through the *Resurrection of the Dead.* The words and actions of man must be of one accord or each deceives themselves. Behold, even those who journey in darkness and unknowing will come to worship at your feet, and will know that I have loved you because I am the indwelling Light within you.

9. Behold, I will make them of the synagogue of Satan, which say they are Jews, and are not, but do lie; behold, I will make them to come and worship before thy feet, and to know that I have loved thee.

10. Because you have tried to be true to my teachings, I am therefore patient and will keep you from the temptations of the flesh which shall come upon the whole of earth. However, those who have not entered into the path of the resurrection must be further imprisoned by worldly temptations, and tried until they also seek oneness with God.

10. Because thou hast kept the word of my patience, I also will keep thee from the hour of temptation, which shall come upon all the world, to try them that dwell upon the earth.

11. Behold, I come quickly. Therefore hold fast to the ways of heaven lest you again be trapped in the captivity of human suffering and lose the crown[2] which serves as a bridge between human and God.

11. Behold I come quickly: hold that fast which thou hast, that no man take thy crown.

12. He that overcomes will become a pillar for the temple of God, which is not built by hands, but comprised of those souls who have surrendered self-will to divine will. They will need to go out no more (re-entry into embodiment). Upon those who have succeeded I shall write the name of my God, *Jehovah,* and name of the city of my God, *New Jerusalem,* (signifying the descent of a spiritual kingdom on earth). And I shall write my new name, Christ, Son of God, on all who have completed the resurrection (transformed human into divine).

12. Him that overcometh will I make a pillar in the temple of my God, and he shall go no more out: and I will write upon him the name of my God and the name of the city of God, which is new Jerusalem, which cometh down out of heaven from my God: and I will write upon him my new name.

13. He who understand these mysteries let him hear my message to the churches.

13 . He that hath an ear, let him hear what the Spirit saith unto the churches.

14. To those of the church of Laodicea, write; These things state the indwelling Christ. I am the Light of the soul, (the first manifestation of creative will of the Father,) and a faithful and true witness of all life existing from the beginning of creation (Genesis 1:2-4).

14. And unto the angel of the church of the Laodiceans write; these things saith the Amen, the faithful and true witness, the beginning of the creation of God.

15. I know your works, and that you are not willing to completely surrender to Divine will; Therefore, you give nothing, for you are neither hot nor cold (one who not centered in God, but is not evil). I wish that you were either hot or cold that I might take those who are ready into the *resurrection of the dead* and leave behind those who still cling to the enticements of human life.

15. I know thy works, that thou art neither cold nor hot: I would thou wert cold or hot.

16. Because you are lukewarm and neither hot nor cold I will deny you entry into the gateway of immortality, for he who gives not the whole of his heart, his mind, and his soul, shall in no way enter the Kingdom of Heaven.

16. So then because thou art lukewarm, and neither cold nor hot, I will spue thee out of my mouth.

17. You claim to be rich and have many possessions and have need for nothing. Yet you are wretched, miserable, poor, blind and naked. Even as you speak you heart follows in the path of worldly enticements. You live in poverty, when you suffer grievous illnesses and fear the dark shadows of death. Your possessions and wealth are not the wealth of God which lives forever, but the wealth of the flesh which is temporal.

17. Because you sayest, I am rich, and increased with goods, and have need of nothing; and knowest not that you art wretched, and miserable, and poor, and blind, and naked.

18. I counsel you to take that which is born of ignorance, intolerance, hatred and deceit, and submit to the purifying fires of the indwelling Christ—that you may know your true wealth. Then you shall be naked no more, and be clothed in white raiment. Anoint[3] your eyes with the wisdom of the ancient ones and darkness shall flee from you, for those things which destroy the body, mind and soul are sore to my eyes.

18. I counsel thee to buy of me gold tried in the fire, that thou mayest be rich; and white raiment, that thou mayest be clothed, and that the shame of thy nakedness do not appear; and anoint thy eyes with eyesalve, that thou mayest see.

19. Although I love those who seek the path to oneness with God, I rebuke and chasten them that they might be purified. Be zealous and seek the path of righteousness that you might be found worthy to enter into the *resurrection* and come before the throne of God.

19. As many as I love, I rebuke and chasten: be zealous therefore, and repent.

20. Behold, I stand at the door which separates self-will from Divine will to assist all who might enter into the *resurrection*. If any human hears the sound of my voice within their soul and chooses the path of Light, I shall descend into them. Then I shall dine with them at the feast of the anointing, (descent of the indwelling Christ to dwell with the soul through transformation). *This is also known as the Feast of the Passover—passing from human to Divine.*

20. Behold, I stand at the door, and knock: if any man hear my voice, and opens the door, I will come in to him, and will sup with him, and he with me.

21. He who overcomes shall rule with me in the Kingdom of God, which governs both heaven and earth. . This is not a place, as you know it, but a state of existence beyond mortal boundaries where those abide who have passed through the resurrection. For as I am risen from matter, so too has the soul overcome the temptations of human weakness.

21. To him that overcometh will I grant to sit with me in my throne, even as I also overcame and am set down with my Father in his throne.

22. He that is able to understand these greater mysteries pertaining to the resurrection let him hear what the Spirit says to the churches.

22. He that hath an ear, let him hear what the Spirit saith unto the churches.

CHAPTER IV

The Four Beasts

Blessed are the pure in heart: for they shall see God

Matthew 5:8

s with every aspect of the Apocalypse, Chapter IV is deeply submerged in the waters of symbolism and it is difficult to find a presentation format which is not cumbersome. However, John is again in Christ, or *cosmic consciousness*, as the chapter opens. This, as previously explained, is a state of pure unity in which the mind of man and the mind of God are united through the indwelling Christ.

Immediately upon entering such a divine glory, John sees the throne of God as it is revealed to the senses. It must be stated in this manner, because God can only appear in personal form through the individual aspect of himself which dwells within the soul. He is pure consciousness abiding in and around all living things and not a deified physical form existing some place in the vast universe. Therefore, He is otherwise invisible except through the expression of nature. Having been called forth by the indwelling Christ to view the things which were yet to come, John sees a heavenly figure sitting on the throne, which he describes "like unto a jasper and sardine stone."

The jasper stone is used as the primary foundation for the Holy City during the dramatic descent of the New Jerusalem in Chapter Twenty-one. It is an opaque and impenetrable gem, signifying the Savior who is placed at the head of all heavenly bodies. The sardine stone, more commonly known as the sardius, is used in the sixth layer of the foundation. While it represents the tribe of Reuben when set in the Hebrew priest's breastplate, here it symbolizes a woman clothed with the sun, or that aspect of the soul which brings forth divine birth indwelling Christ out of the tomb of human darkness. This refers to the balancing of human and divine will.

Thus, John beholds God (Savior & Son) who will lift his soul out of its ignorant state through Divine Will. John also speaks of a rainbow around the throne. Pure white light will produce a prism effect of a rainbow (i.e., the full spectrum of light displayed in its individual facets), and, therefore, symbolizes the whole, or one Light expressing through all realms. John states that it is a sight like unto an emerald, an ancient symbol of the indwelling Christ, which rises from the body of the beast into the mystical union. It is decreed that anyone wishing to stand before the throne of God must first unite the soul with its indwelling Christ counterpart (the two natures in divine union-2) or it cannot be released from its imprisonment to matter (4 elements ruling over the sentient being. 2-4).

Around the throne there is thunder and lightning. In this case thunder designates the dismantling (shaking loose) of false concepts, while lightning expresses the descent of sporadic interludes of great illumination. There are also seven burning lamps before the throne of God, which John states are the seven spirits of God, or the seven forces of cosmic law. Next he describes the four beasts which guard the throne: the lion (Divine birth), the calf (sacrifice), the face of man (surrender) and the flying eagle (ascension). These have eyes both before and behind, to represent the past and the future.

Although it has been conventionally believed and taught that a person can be made pure through the acceptance of Jesus Christ, this can be a bit misleading. God has dwelled within the individual expression of human life since its inception, and He has not only instilled the soul's purpose during its process of systematic progression, but has also witnessed all thoughts and actions performed by the soul during this evolutionary process. Now that it stands before His throne, the impure soul cannot approach too closely because the throne is guarded by four beasts. Each beast represents an aspect of purification to be accomplished before the state of unity can prevail. As the lion connotes first born, it has been decreed that the soul must first give birth to, or raise, the indwelling Christ.

Next the soul must sacrifice its attachments for the outside world, as the calf signifies immolation. Sacrifice of a yearling calf was considered the highest of gifts in ancient times, thus representing the soul's surrender of its long enslavement to its earthly abode. After these things have been accomplished, human will concedes to Divine will, for the face of mortality must take upon itself the *face of divinity*. This transformation of human into divine, however, cannot be accomplished before raising from mortality as the eagle, the final beast. The eagle represents ascension in Christian literature, thus the soul has now been born anew in order to ascend to the heavenly abode wherein the throne of God stands.

Because the soul has been bound to earth, enmeshed in worldly things, governed by self-will, and is unaware of its divine inheritance, the four beasts of the apocalypse each bear six wings, designating the first six periods, or epochs, of systematic progression according to Mosaic teachings. (See Genesis 1:27-31). However, as each beast is overcome through the remarkable transformation of human to divine, the soul is united with its divine counterpart (2) and liberated from anthropoid entanglement (4 elements). Therefore, it is no longer governed by terrestrial life, but governed by celestial forces which direct the pre-destined progress of the universe.

1. After this I looked, and beheld the doorway between my soul and the heavenly kingdom was opened. And the voice of Alpha and Omega (first voice) called me forth as by trumpet, saying, Come up here and I will show those things which must come to pass when all people enter into the resurrection and earth as you know it, passes away.

1. After this I looked, and behold, a door was opened in heaven: and the first voice which I heard was as it were of a trumpet talking with me; which said, Come up hither, and I will shew thee things which must be hereafter.

2. The consciousness of my human nature began to ebb, and my soul, one with the indwelling Christ, began to expand, until I was no more bound by flesh. I became one in the Infinite and behold, a throne was set in heaven and figure sat on the throne.

2. And immediately I was in the spirit: and, behold a throne was set in heaven, and one sat on the throne.

3. He was like a jasper (signifying ruler over all heavenly flocks) and a sardine stone (signifying executioner of Divine will). His countenance was as the sun, which broke into prisms around the throne like a rainbow, in sight like an emerald (signifying eternal life).

3. And he that sat was to look upon like a jasper and a sardine stone: and there was a rainbow round about the throne, in sight like unto an emerald.

4. Around the throne were four (four and twenty seats; and upon the seats I saw four (four elements) and twenty elders sitting, (the indwelling Christ and the Soul must become one in order to stand in the presence of the throne 2-0).These were the four elements, or forces, designated to rule over matter, which have bound the indwelling Christ and the soul to mortality. None can come before the throne of God who has not triumphed over their elemental nature (crowns of gold) by passing through the fires of purification.

4. And round about the throne were four and twenty seats: and upon the seats I saw four and twenty elders sitting, clothed in white raiment; and they had on their heads crowns of gold.

5. And out of the throne proceeded great interludes of revelation, and those things still impure within the soul were shaken loose as by thunder. After this I saw seven lamps burning before the throne, representing the seven forces of cosmic law.

5. And out of the throne proceeded lightning and thunderings and voices: and there were seven lamps of fire burning before the throne, which are the seven Spirits of God.

6. Before the throne there was a sea of glass like crystal (mirror—heaven over earth). Around the throne were four beasts, signifying four transformational changes which must take place within the soul before it can become one with the indwelling Christ and approach the throne of God. The beasts were full of eyes before and behind, for they were the multitude on earth who has been and who is, and who has not entered into the resurrection.

6. And before the throne there was a sea of glass like unto crystal: and in the midst of the throne, and round about the throne, were four beasts full of eyes before and behind.

7. These four beasts serve as guardians of the throne and deny the soul entry into heaven until it has raised the indwelling Christ (lion-first born), surrendered its attachment to worldly ways (calf-sacrifice), acquiesced to Divine will (face of man), and in unity rises as savior incarnate (eagle-messiah, or savior).[1]

7. And the first beast was like a lion, and the second beast like a calf, and the third beast had a face as a man, and the fourth beast was like a flying eagle.

8. The four beasts each had six wings (bound by the four elements to the sixth epoch of progression - human). These are the multitudes which have not passed into the resurrection. The beasts rest not day or night, saying, Holy, holy, holy, Lord God Almighty, which was, and is, and is yet to come.

8. And the four beasts had each of them six wings about him; and they were full of eyes within: and they rest not day and night, saying Holy, holy, holy, Lord God Almighty, which was, and is, and is to come.

9. When the soul has been purified through rebirth, sacrifice, surrender and ascension, it shall give glory, and honor, and thanks to Him that sits on the throne who lives forever.

9. And when those beasts give glory and honour and thanks to him that sat on the throne, who liveth forever and ever.

10. The two selves, the indwelling Christ, and the soul, having become one, will be liberated from human bondage (four elements), and fall down before God to worship Him, saying:

10. The four and twenty elders fall before him that sat on the throne, and worship him that liveth forever and ever, and cast their crowns before the throne saying,

11. "You are worthy, O Lord, to receive glory and honor and power; for you created all things and for their glory were they created. (God is omnipotent and omniscient and does not possess emotions. He created life as a gift unto itself.)

11. Thou art worthy, O Lord, to receive glory and honour and power: for thou hast created all things, and for thy pleasure they are and were created.

CHAPTER V

Book of Time

Through His mysterious wonder light is come into my heart;
mine eye has set its gaze on everlasting things. He has given
us an inheritance in the lot of the Holy Beings, and
joined us in communion with the sons of Heaven.

Hymn of the Initiates,
Dead Sea Scriptures 1-41:15, Gaster

The stage is set in Chapter V to open the seven seals and let loose the four horses of the apocalypse. It begins as John sees God sitting upon a throne and holding a mysterious book in his right hand. It is important to remember that the throne room is located within the nature of every human being and that it is the individualized aspect of God within the soul, referred to as the Son, or indwelling Christ. The book is held in the right hand and signifies righteousness, in that the right hand is generally the primary worker in all physical action. Therefore, that which is noble, good, hardworking and pure is placed on the right hand of God, while the left hand, which usually functions as a support system, denotes that which is weaker and subject to mortality. Although the book represents seven epochs of soul regeneration as outlined in Genesis 1 & 2, particular emphasis will

45

be placed upon the seventh and final seal because it deals with the resurrection of the dead, or the raising of divine man from the throes of human maturation.

It comes to pass that none without embodiment, none who dwell in ignorance (although in a physical body), nor any creature which is lower than man can open the book. It cannot be opened because the book connotes the soul which has passed through six progressive states of necessity, but is not yet divine. The elder (spiritual counterpart and that which reveals the mysteries) tells John not to weep over the dark ignorance of human life, for the indwelling Christ in mankind, or that aspect of God incarcerated within the soul in the beginning, has prevailed to open the book and to loose the seven seals.

After these words have been spoken to him, the apostle sees the resurrected Christ appear in the center of the throne as a sacrificial lamb, to portend his surrender to human bondage throughout the seven phases of earthly progression (seven horns). Having been relegated to this role by God in the beginning, the newly risen Christ and master of the soul assures salvation to all who come to him. As he steps forth to open the book, he also bears the seven powers of cosmic law which will purify the whole of earth. When he does so; the obstacles that have forbidden the soul entry into the divine state falls away, or surrenders, before Him.

Each of the beasts and elders holds harps and golden vials which are filled with the prayers of saints. In the ancient Hebrew mysteries the harp was regarded as a secret symbol of human constitution: The body of the instrument—the physical form; the strings—the nerves; and the musician—the Spirit. By playing through the nerves, the Creator establishes the harmonies of normal life function in matter. These obviously become discordant if any of the natural and cosmic laws are defiled, and the soul then suffers reprisals because of its ignorance. Rabbinical tradition asserts that the harp was called noble because it was like the body rounded out and covered with skin.

The elders not only bear harps, but also hold golden vials. Gold, as previously outlined, represents both the spiritual nature of the soul and wisdom. Therefore, the vials signify containers of wisdom, which will purify the carnality accumulated through mankind's cycles of evolutionary necessity.

There is little to add to this chapter, for most of the symbolic material has been thoroughly covered in previous explanations. However, the balance can be summed up by saying that the indwelling Christ, having been incapacitated through human progression (slain) will transform that which is terrestrial into that which is celestial (redeemed). At this time John is shown that those who will enter into the resurrection will number ten thousand times ten thousand, and thousands and thousands. While there is no specific mention here of the one hundred forty-four thousand, most scholars are inclined to view it in that manner. Actually, the one hundred forty-four thousand implies that the soul which has been imprisoned by the four elements and the indwelling Christ which has also been imprisoned in matter (4-4) must become one (1) through the union of the body, soul, and spirit (000). This will be discussed in greater detail in Chapter VII.

As Chapter V concludes, one is left with an optimistic view; that once the soul has raised the indwelling Christ, he will rule forever.

1. And I saw a book in the right hand of God, who sat upon the throne. It signified the seven epochs or cycles of the soul's journey through matter, for it was sealed with seven seals.

1. And I saw in the right hand of him that sat on the throne a book written within and on the backside, sealed with seven seals.

2. And I saw an angel (same symbolic meaning as the first beast, for only those who have raised the indwelling Christ can view the contents of the book) proclaiming in a loud voice, Who is worthy to open the book, and to loose the seals.

2. And I saw a strong angel proclaiming with a loud voice, Who is worthy to open the book, and to loose the seals thereof?

3. And no one without embodiment, nor in the body, or any life form not yet human, was worthy to open the book, or look upon it, for they has not yet raised the indwelling Christ and entered into the resurrection.

3. And no man in heaven, nor in earth, neither under the earth, was able to open the book, neither to look thereon.

4. And I wept, because the impurities of the soul prohibited it from partaking of that which was written in the book.

4. And I wept much, because no man was found worthy to open and to read the book, neither to look thereon.

5. The first elder, (see verse 2) said, "Do not weep, for the Christ in mankind is able to open the seven seals. He is the first born[1] and comes forth in the sign of David. (Six pointed star representing the soul's descent into matter and its ascent from worldly attachments—Star of David)

5. And one of the elders saith unto me, Weep not: behold, the Lion of the tribe of Judah, the Root of David, hath prevailed to open the book, and to loose the seven seals thereof.

6. I beheld, and lo, from the throne of God, came forth a lamb, (a symbol of the indwelling Christ, having been slain by his descent into evolutionary darkness. He was now raised from the flesh, and contained within him the seven epochs of progressive evolution (horns) and bore the seven forces of cosmic law.

6. And I beheld, and, lo, in the midst of the throne and of the four beasts, and in the midst of the elders, stood a Lamb as it has been slain, having seven horns and seven eyes, which are the seven Spirits of God sent forth into all the earth.

7. And the resurrected and indwelling Christ came and took the book from the right hand of God.

7. And he came and took the book out of the right hand of him that sat upon the throne.

8. And when he had taken the book, the soul, having raised the dead (Christ—Lion), sacrificed its corporeal nature (sacrifice—calf), surrendered human will (face of man) and ascended (eagle), became like unto a harp, that Will of God might pour forth His wisdom (golden vials) over the soul's worldly nature.

8. And when he had taken the book, the four beasts and four and twenty elders fell down before the Lamb, having everyone of them harps, and golden vials full of odours, which are the prayers of saints.

9. And they sang a new song to the lamb. "You alone are worthy to open the Ark of the Covenant within the soul and reveal the great mysteries thereof, for you who were slain have been raised from the dead. Through your sacrifice[2] (blood), you have redeemed the souls of every kindred, and tongue, and nation."

9. And they sung a new song, saying, Thou art worthy to take the book, and to open the seals thereof: for thou wast slain, and hat redeemed us to God by thy blood out of every kindred, and tongue, and people, and nation;

10. He who he has been raised in mankind, transforms them into kings and priests before God. It is he, who shall rule over all the earth through mankind because of his holy union with every soul in the world.

10. And hast made us unto our God kings and priests: and we shall reign on the earth.

11. And I beheld and I heard the voice of many angels (those who have been transformed from human into divine through surrender of their mortality, because of their union with the indwelling Christ—lamb), and the number of them included every man, woman, and child who had entered into the resurrection.

11. And I beheld, and I heard the voice of many angels round about the throne, and the beasts, and the elders: and the number of them was ten thousand times ten thousand, and thousands of thousands

12. No longer were there voices raised in dissension, for the multitudes were now of one accord and they said in a loud voice, "Worthy is the Son of God, Lamb of the most high, who dwells within every soul, to receive power and riches, and wisdom and strength, and honor and glory.

12. Saying with a loud voice, Worthy is the Lamb that was slain to receive power, and riches, and wisdom, and strength, and honour, and glory, and blessing.

13. And every creature without embodiment, those who walked upon the earth, and those living things not yet human, and creatures of the sea, were subject God and to his Son who dwelled in them. They said, "Blessing and honor, and glory, let power be given to Him who rules over all life, and glory be to the indwelling Christ who has risen in every soul, for he shall reign without end."

13. And every creature which is in heaven, and on the earth, and under the earth, and such as are in the sea, and all that are in them, heard I saying, Blessing, and honour, and glory, and power, be unto him that sitteth upon the throne and unto the Lamb forever and ever.

14. And the soul and the indwelling Christ having risen and been freed from the earthly chains which bound it, worshipped Him who lived forever and ever.

14. And the four beasts said, Amen: And the four and twenty elders fell down and worshipped him that liveth forever and ever.

So, for mine own part, molded of clay
that I am, with an heart of stone, lo, of what worth
am I, that I should attain unto this?
Yet, behold, Thou has set Thy word in this ear of dust,
and graven upon this heart eternal realities;
and Thou hast brought to an end all of my
forwardness, to bring me
into covenant with Thee that I may stand
before thee evermore
unshaken in the glow of the Perfect Light,
where no darkness is
for ever, and where all is peace
unbounded until the end of time.

Book of Hymns, XVIII
The Dead Sea Scriptures
Gaster

CHAPTER VI

Horses of the Apocalypse

*O God, thou art my God; early will I seek thee: my soul
thirsteth for thee, my flesh longeth for thee in a dry and
thirsty land, where no water is; To see thy power and
thy glory, so as I have seen thee in the sanctuary.*

Psalms 63: 1-2

The thundering hooves of the four horses of the apocalypse stampede across the pages as the drama builds in the sixth chapter. It is interesting to note that most scholars have given more attention to verses two through nine of this segment of St. John's Revelation, than they have to the opening of the seventh seal which consumes all of chapters eight and nine. Even when the apocalyptic quadrupeds have vanished there still remains the seventh angel of the seventh seal with seven vials, whose mystery is not revealed until chapter seventeen. Obviously, John the Beloved relegated only four verses to the horses of the Apocalypse, but wrote a great deal more concerning the opening of the final seal. One must therefore assume that the latter is of greater importance and approach this particular sequence of verses accordingly.

53

By this time, it is clear that mankind must pass through the resurrection of the dead, or raise that divine aspect of God (Christ) which dwells in him to everlasting glory. Only through this profound transformation can the soul hope to become one with God. As Chapter VI begins, John, who has accomplished this mystery of mysteries, sees the risen Christ open one of the seals. Since thunder always precedes a storm and creates the preconditions for lightning, signifying certain illuminating experiences in the apocalypse, the opening is as the noise of thunder. Then one of the four beasts says, "Come and see." This is the first beast, the lion, for there is a distinct correlation between the beasts and the horses. As the lion represents first born, then the horse, which is white, represents the birth of the Light of God in mankind. This is further substantiated by the fact that the horse bears a rider holding a bow and crown, indicating war and rulership. He has been sent forth to conquer. Thus the stage is set for the indwelling Christ to champion his bride (soul) by assisting her in the battle to overcome her bondage to matter, thereby redeeming his heavenly abode wherein he is the sovereign ruler.

After the second seal is opened the calf says, "Come and see." It is natural to assume that the second beast is the calf, because it emblemizes sacrifice and surrender of the corporeal nature, and the horse is red. John chose to use the color red because it represents bloodshed, sacrifice, and war. And power was given to him that sat upon the horse to take peace from earth, that they should kill one another, and there was given to him a great sword.

When the soul has pierced the inner sanctuary and raised the indwelling Christ it must battle and defeat the corporeal nature with the famous sword of truth and justice. (See 1:16). There can be no peace now, for the material ways which have drawn the soul deeply into the world of matter must die before the unified state (marriage to the lamb) can be consummated. Subsequently, the third seal is opened and the third beast, the face of Divine will, says, "Come and see." And John the Beloved beheld a black horse;

and he that sat on him had a pair of balances in his hand. In that the third beast represents the surrender of self-will to Divine will, the horse is black, for the soul must surrender to the edicts of the indwelling Christ. The balances indicate that the soul must now stand trial before the indwelling Christ and receive just retribution for deeds both good and evil.

Revelation 6:9 gives some indication of how judgment will be rendered, because the voice of the third beast says, "*A measure of wheat for a penny, and three measures of barley for a penny; and see that you hurt not the oil and wine.*"

Wheat was once looked upon as a succulent grain and held in high esteem, and it is used in this verse to signify the good deeds of the soul. Barley, however, was sometimes mixed with cheap grains and often considered part of the price of an adulteress, or a lewd woman, thereby expressing low rank and poverty. Therefore, John selects barley to represent the indiscretions which the soul has committed. This can be summed up by saying that all humans, upon raising the dead, will enter a period of atonement in which they shall reap what they have sown. Although purification is rendered accordingly, God has decreed that the oil and wine shall not be hurt. These both symbolize the spiritual nature of the soul; oil because it was used for anointing and looked upon as the embodiment of God, or descent of God to live in the flesh; and wine, because it was the pure essence of the grape after it has been crushed, thus becoming synonymous with purgation, or judgment.

When the fourth seal is opened, the voice of the fourth beast, the eagle, says, "Come and see." After this John sees a pale horse; and the name of him who sat upon the horse was death and hell followed him. Power was given to them to kill a fourth part of the earth with a sword, with hunger, and with death. The fourth beast signifies rebirth of the inner divinity of mankind from the ashes of mortality, so the pale horse proclaims death to the human passions which have led mankind into darkness and ignorance, as well as starvation to the injurious desires of the flesh. Transformation of the soul from human to divine has now been broken into four precise patterns of metamorphosis. Death to the fourth part of the world merely means ascension through purification as expressed by the fourth beast and fourth horse.

Immediately thereafter, the fifth seal is opened and John sees the souls under the altar (doorway between heaven and earth) which have already passed through the resurrection of the dead because they were true to the teachings pertaining to the mysteries of transformation. As they have sacrificed their lives to serve this great cause, they ask God how long it will be before the rest of the world is purged of its carnality. At this time, the lives which they have given for truth will be avenged because their teachings would be instrumental in drawing all people into the kingdom of heaven. In Revelation 6:11, the illumined, the elect (white robes), are comforted and told that they should remain in the heavenly kingdom until the corporeal nature of all humans has been slain.

As the sixth seal is opened, John beholds a great earthquake (the soul and all its memories are shaken loose) and the sun (the world of corporeality) became black as sackcloth made of goat's hair, and the moon (mind) became as blood. Then the stars (false aspirations) fell from heaven and the heaven is parted as a scroll and every mountain (false ideals) is moved out of its place, signaling the soul's entry into the resurrection.

Through devotional surrender, whether through meditation, love, service, or prayer, there will come a time when every soul becomes submerged in the consciousness of God. No longer restricted by its fleshly counterpart, the soul is opened like the womb of a mother giving birth to a child. In this state of unity the power and consciousness of God is like a mighty earthquake, for He pours great revelations into the soul which shakes it like wind blowing upon a leaf. Girded in sackcloth (great tribulation) the soul sees all that it has done to others and judgment descends upon it, that it might be judged as it has judged others. There will be no peace until the mighty Armageddon battle is over, for the Light of God is closed off, as a door shuts in darkness. The moon (symbol of the mind) becomes as blood because of its suffering and false ideals, human aspirations, and self-will; it falls upon the corporeal nature, even as stars fall from the sky.

As verses 15, 16, & 17 unfold, it becomes apparent that no human being will be excluded from the transfiguration, and there is no place to hide. Although this probably seems more frightening than the traditional apocalyptic approach, it should not be so. Human beings have already proven that they cannot control their unruly and often violent nature alone, for they fight on the battlefields, foster and spread diseases, become enfeebled by their own dissipative habits, and create dissension with those they love. However, once they have entered into the resurrection of the dead, all impurities are purged by the risen Christ; much like a threshing machine separates the wheat from the chaff.

When the soul finally understands it true nature as well as its purpose, it enters into the peace it has sought since the beginning. Therefore, Chapter VI does not reveal something frightening, but a glorious awakening in which human nature is transformed. It also heralds the beginning of the mighty battle which will wreak its miracle on the whole of earth.

1. When the first seal was opened, the sound was like thunder (heralding the opening of the first seal). The lion, which is guardian of the throne and signifies the resurrection of the indwelling Christ states, "Come and see."

1. And I saw when the Lamb opened one of the seals, and I heard, as it were the noise of thunder, one of the four beasts saying, Come and see.

2. Behold the indwelling Christ rides forth on a white horse (signifying the illumined mind, or descent of the Spirit to live in the flesh),[1] and he carries a bow that he might war against the impurities which inhabit the soul, and rule in heaven and over earth.

2. And I saw, and behold a white horse: and he that sat on him had a bow; and a crown was given unto him: And he went forth conquering and to conquer.

3. After this the second seal was opened and the calf (sacrifice) said, "Come and see."

3. And when he had opened the second seal, I heard the second beast say, Come and see.

4. Then I beheld the indwelling Christ sitting on a red horse to signify that the soul must sacrifice its corporeal enticements for the sake of the lamb. And he was given a mighty sword of truth and justice to destroy the peace of the soul until all of its impurities had been slain.

4. And there went out another horse that was red: and power was given to him that sat thereon to take peace from the earth, and that they should kill one another: and there was given unto him a great sword.

5. When the third seal had been opened, I heard the third beast (Divine will), say, "Come and see." And I beheld the indwelling Christ come forth on a black horse. He had a pair of balances to weigh the good and evil of the soul, for the time of atonement was at hand.

5. And when he had opened the third seal, I heard the third beast say, Come and see, And I beheld and lo a black horse; and he that sat on him had a pair of balances in his hands.

6. And I heard a voice in the midst of the four beasts say, "A measure of wheat for a penny (good deeds of the soul during its sojourn in matter), and three measures of barley for a penny (iniquitous actions of the soul during its sojourn in matter), but hurt not that which is anointed (oil) and divine (wine)."[2]

6. And I heard a voice in the midst of the four beasts say, A measure of wheat for a penny, and three measures of barley for a penny; and three measures of barley for a penny; and see thou hurt not the oil and the wine.

7. As the fourth seal was opened, I heard the voice of the eagle (ascension) say to me, "Come and see."

7. And when he had opened the fourth seal, I heard the voice of the fourth beast say, come and see.

8. The indwelling Christ came riding forth on a pale horse signifying death to the soul's final attachment to matter, and hell followed him. The soul must now enter the gateway of perdition, and the defiled aspects, because of its worldly ways, will be killed by truth and justices in order that it ascend.

8. And I looked, and behold a pale horse: and his name that sat on him was Death, and Hell followed with him. And power was given unto them over the fourth part of the earth, to kill with sword, and with hunger, and with death, and with the beasts of the earth.

9. And when the fifth seal was opened, I saw beneath the bridge (altar) which separates self-will from Divine will,[3] the souls of the resurrected whose corporeal natures had already been slain because they had entered into the resurrection.

10. They cried with a loud voice, saying, "How long, O Lord, will it be before you come forth in all mankind to purify the whole earth, that our work with the people not be lost?"

11. And the souls of those who had already entered the resurrection were made pure (white robes) and it was said to them, "Rest in this land until earth has been redeemed. Your fellow servants and all mankind must be killed as you were killed before the world can be redeemed."

12. Then, I beheld the indwelling Christ open the sixth seal, and there was a great upheaval in the soul. And the *dark night* (see St. John of the Cross—Dark Night of the Soul) covered the soul with sackcloth and it was judged according to its good and evil. And the mind (moon) became as blood and it repented over its iniquitous actions.

9. And when he had opened the fifth seal, I saw under the altar the souls of them that were slain for the word of God, and for the testimony which they held.

10. And they cried with a loud voice, saying, How long, O Lord, holy and true, dost thou not judge and avenge our blood on them that dwell on the earth?

11. And white robes were given unto every one of them; and it was said unto them, that they should rest yet for a little season, until their fellow servants also and their brethren, that should be killed as they were, should be fulfilled.

12. And I beheld when he had opened the sixth seal, and, lo, there was a great earthquake; and the sun became black as sackcloth of hair, and the moon became as blood.

13. And the false ideals and aspirations (stars) of the soul fell away like ash, as a fig tree which cast away those figs which are not firmly attached when it is shaken before the wind.

13. And the stars of heaven fell unto the earth, even as a fig tree casteth her untimely figs, when she is shaken of a mighty wind.

14. The Light of God was shut away from the soul as a scroll when it has been rolled together, and every false human indiscretion and uncleanness was moved out of the body, mind and soul.

14. And the heaven departed as a scroll when it is rolled together; and every mountain and island were moved out of their place.

15. None escapes the quagmire of their past indiscretions, not the rulers of nations, statesmen, rich people, chiefs, the influential, administrators, or the free. In the hour of darkness, all souls will seek asylum from their unrighteousness through the outer world of the senses.

15. And the kings of the earth, and the great men, and the rich men, and the chief captains, and the mighty men, and every bondman and every free man, hid themselves in the rocks of the mountains;

16. In this same hour the soul will seek escape from God's retributions and the wrath of the indwelling Christ, by attempting to return to its corporeal nature.

16. And said to the mountains and rocks, Fall on us, and hide us from the face of him that sitteth on the throne, and from the wrath of the Lamb:

17. But the great Day of Atonement (Armageddon) has come and no human being can escape purification.

17. For the great day of his wrath is come; and who shall be able to stand.

Angel of the Four Winds

So also is the resurrection of the dead. It is sown in
corruption; it is raised in incorruption: It is sown
in dishonour; it is raised in glory: it is sown in weakness;
it is raised in power: It is sown a natural body; it
is raised a spiritual body. There is a natural
body, and there is a spiritual body.

I Corinthians 15:42-44

Chapter seven may well be considered one of the most touching chapters in the Apocalypse. Although the groundwork is still being laid for a terrible battle to unfold upon the opening of the seventh seal there is a subtle promise which is equaled only in Chapter 8.

The seventh book opens with the appearance of four angels, signifying the four seasons standing on the four cardinal points of earth: east, south, west and north. Each angel holds the four winds, or elements, (earth, water, air and fire) which will purify mankind. It is written in this manner because spring is equated with the east, or new birth; summer, south and prime of life; fall, west and middle age; and winter, north, old age and dying. As before, the meaning of the four angels correlates to the four beasts around

the throne of God and the four horses of the apocalypse, because
the symbolism refers to the soul's transformation from human to
divine (rebirth, sacrifice, surrender and ascension). Another ingredient, however, has been added, this time, i.e., the four elements consisting of earth, water, fire and air. The body, of course,
must be purified by water, representing the purifying process which
brings the soul into harmony with the laws of nature. Then it
must be purged by means of fire (Light) which will destroy all of
the inconsistencies which are not in harmony with God and the
laws of the cosmos. When this transformation is completed the
newborn soul can then ascend to its heavenly abode, or estate,
like the mighty eagle (air).

Another angel ascends from the east (new birth) bringing the
seal of the living God (i.e., the resurrection of the indwelling Christ
and the descent of the Spirit to live in the flesh). He cries aloud to
the four angels standing on the four cardinal points of the universe, who holds judgment over earth that they shall not hurt the
body (earth), the mind (sea), or the soul (see tree of life), until
those who are prepared for the resurrection of the dead have been
sealed with the mark of God on their foreheads. As the angel has
risen from the east, the mark must be that of the eastern star, or
the sign of David, a six pointed symbol representing the descent
of spirit to live in the flesh (downward interlocking V), and spirit's
return to its heavenly abode (upward interlocking V). (See 3:28.)

Thereafter, John heard "*the number of them which were sealed*";
and there were 144,000, or the twelve tribes of Israel. This is a
very fascinating statement, particularly in view of the fact that
Christendom commonly believes that by accepting Jesus as their
savior they are included in this number. That belief, however, is
based on a literal interpretation. The 144,000, as mentioned in
the Introduction, is considerably more complex than this because
it relates to a specific level of consciousness rather than a quantity.
As alluded to in 6:11, the indwelling Christ, by his descent into
matter, became bound by the four elements through the soul's

affinity to worldly ways. (Indwelling Christ bound to matter by the four elements—4 and soul bound to matter by the four elements—4=44.) As previously mentioned, these two aspects must become united, to be one with God. Finally the body, mind & soul are each represented by a single zero, or circle, signifying without end and continuum (000). In summary, the soul cannot become one in God except through marriage with the indwelling Christ.

The code pertaining to the twelve tribes of Israel defies translation without an understanding of the Mosaic mysteries, many of which are evident in the subsequent Christian mysteries. As with all of the preceding material, nothing is exactly as it seems. This applies not only to the twelve tribes of Israel, but also to the number 12,000. Although there were twelve sons born to Jacob/Israel and his wives during Egypt's eighteenth dynasty and early reign of the New Empire, the sun had set upon their graves over two hundred years before Jesus's predecessor, Moses, was born.

The descendants of the sons of Jacob followed Moses into the wilderness during the month of Xanthicaus (March-April) on the fifteenth day of the lunar month, four hundred and thirty years after Abraham entered Canaan. How many really left Egypt is unknown, but there is no reason to doubt the fact that the tribes were separated according to tribal lineage in order to relegate responsibility. It is at this point that the number 12,000 is first used, signifying the marriage (1) of the indwelling Christ and the soul.. It cannot be a coincidence that there are also twelve signs of the zodiac, twelve months of the year, twelve hours of a day, twelve hours of night, twelve stones in the Hebrew breast plate, and twelve layers to the wall of the new Jerusalem (see 21:20).

The twelve tribes symbolized a vanguard destined to unite heaven and earth, and to bring forth a world based upon natural and cosmic law. With Moses as the center (as a sun is a center), the twelve tribes reflect the perfect movement of cosmic order after the manner of the rotation of the solar system around the earth's sun. As John's vision continues, he sees the ultimate perfection of all people through the symbolism of the twelve tribes of Israel which laid a basic foundation for the brotherhood of mankind. This is further substantiated as John sees a great multitude in Rev. 9, "*Which no man could number.*" Within this multitude were all nations, relatives, peoples, and different languages. They stand with the purified souls before the indwelling Christ, carrying palm branches to signify victory over death.

After this segment of the drama has unfolded, the first elder (1) looks at John and asks, "What are these who are arrayed in white robes and where did they come from?"

This question does not confound John, who has undergone the transformation of human to divine, and he replies, "Sir, you know."

The four final verses of this episode of the Apocalypse reflect the very core of its purpose and its story, and establishes the beauty of the soul's transformation from human to divine. As the elder responds to John's statement, he states that these are the resurrected, those who have passed through the dark night of tribulation and have purified their souls by union to the indwelling Christ through the sacrifice of their corporeal nature. They can now stand before the throne of God and serve him day and night in his temple, and He shall dwell among them. They shall no more know hunger or thirst, or again be drawn into the world of matter, for they shall be taught from the eternal waters of wisdom, and there shall be no more tears or sorrow.

1. After these things I saw four angels (seasons) on the four cardinal points of earth, holding the four elements (earth, water, fire and air) to purify the body, the mind and the soul of every living being that they might be reborn.

1. And after these things I saw four angels standing on the four corners of the earth, holding the four winds of the earth, that the wind should not blow on the earth, nor on the sea, nor on any tree.

2. And I saw the star (sign of David) of new birth (east) and insignia of God, upon the souls of those who had been called forth to be judged. Then the Angel of the East, signifying birth of the indwelling Christ in humanity, cried in a loud voice to the four elements which were given judgment over the body (earth) and the mind (sea).

2. And I saw another angel ascending from the east, having the seal of the living God: and he cried with a loud voice to the four angels, to whom it was given to hurt the earth and the sea.

3. Saying, "Hurt not the body, neither the mind, nor the soul (trees- divine principles within the soul, i.e. a tree raises its branches toward heaven), until the soul has brought forth the inner Christ."

3. Saying, Hurt not the earth, neither the sea, nor the trees, till we have sealed the servants of our God in their foreheads.

4. Then, I saw the indwelling Christ, which had been restricted by his descent into matter, to dwell in the soul (4), and the soul which had been drawn deeply into matter by its attraction to worldly life (4—see forward), become one in God (1) through the union of the body, mind and soul. And these are represented by the twelve tribes of Israel (twelve phases of trans-formation the soul passes through as it fights ego and self-will).[1]

4. And I heard the number of them which were sealed: and there were sealed an hundred and forty and four thousand of all the tribes of the children of Israel.

5. And those aspects in the soul, symbolized by the tribe of Judah (first-born), the tribe of Reuben (illumination), and the tribe of Gad (humility-surrender), were established during the resurrection that the soul might become one in God through union with the inner Christ.

5. Of the tribe of Judah were sealed twelve thousand. Of the tribe of Reuben were sealed twelve thousand. Of the tribe of Reuben were sealed twelve thousand. Of the tribe of Gad were sealed twelve thousand.

6. And those aspects of the soul as represented by the tribe Aser (soul rising from the body of the beast), the tribe of Nephthalim (death of the ego), and tribe of Manasses (repentance & retribution), were established during the resurrection, that the soul might become one in God through union with the inner Christ.

6. Of the tribe of Aser were sealed twelve thousand. Of the tribe of Nephthalim were sealed twelve thousand. Of the tribe of Manasses were sealed twelve thousand.

7. And all the tribe of Simeon (purification), the tribe of Levi (wisdom), and the tribe of Issachar (peace—the separation of the soul from the indwelling Christ that it might be subject to his will), was wrought in the soul that it might become one in God through union with the inner Christ.

7. Of the tribe of Simeon were sealed twelve thousand. Of the tribe of Levi were sealed twelve thousand. Of the tribe of Issachar were sealed twelve thousand.

8. And all the people in the tribe of Zabulon (justice), and tribe of Joseph (desert/desolation—the final death struggle of the ego), and the tribe of Benjamin (victory—rulership of the Christ over mortality).

8. Of the tribe of Zabulon were sealed twelve thousand. Of the tribe of Joseph were sealed twelve thousand. Of the tribe of Benjamin were sealed twelve thousand.

9. After this I beheld, and, lo, a great multitude which no man could number, of all nations and kindreds and people and languages, raised the indwelling Christ and stood with purified souls before the throne of God carrying palms to signify victory over mortality (death).

9. After this I beheld, and, lo, a great multitude, which no man could number, of all nations, and kindreds, and people, and tongues, stood before the throne, and before the Lamb, clothed with white robes, and palms in their hands.

10. And they cried with a loud voice, saying, "We have been redeemed by God who sits upon the throne through the resurrection of the indwelling Christ.

10. And cried with a loud voice, saying, Salvation to our God which sitteth upon the throne, and unto the Lamb.

11. And the souls who had become one in God through the resurrection of the inner Christ by sacrificing their corporeal natures and surrender of self-will, fell on their faces and worshipped God (see 4:4).

11. And all the angels stood round about the throne, and about the elders and the four beasts, and fell before the throne on their faces, and worshipped God.

12. Saying, "Amen: Blessing, and glory, and wisdom, and thanksgiving and honor, and power, and might to our God who will live for ever and ever."

12. Saying, Amen: Blessing, and glory, and wisdom, and thanksgiving, and honour, and power, and might, be unto our God forever and ever. Amen.

13. The first elder (see 5:5), asked me, "What are these who are arrayed in white robes and from where do they come/"

13. And one of the elders answered, saying unto me, What are these which are arrayed in white robes? and whence come they?

14. I said to him, "Sir, you know." He replied, saying, "These are those who have entered into the resurrection of the dead and raised the indwelling Christ. Their souls have been purified and made white by sacrifice and surrender of self-will.

14. And I said unto him, Sir, thou knowest. And he said to me, These are they which came out of great tribulation, and have washed their robes, and made them white in the blood of the Lamb.

15. "Now they have come before the throne of God and will serve Him day and night in His temple which has now been raised within them; And he that sits upon the throne shall dwell among them forever.

15. Therefore are they before the throne of God, and serve him day and night in his temple: and he that sitteth on the throne shall dwell among them.

16. "They shall never again know hunger or thirst, nor have need of the sun to light on them, nor heat to warm them,*(for they shall go no more out)*.

16. They shall hunger no more, neither thirst any more; neither shall the sun light on them, nor any heat.

17, "For the indwelling Christ who has been resurrected in them shall care for them, and lead them to the living waters of truth and wisdom forever. And God shall wipe away the tears from their eyes (see clearly).

17. For the Lamb which is in the midst of the throne shall feed them, and shall lead them unto living fountains of waters, and God shall wipe away all tears from their eyes.

CHAPTER VIII

The Seventh Seal

For ye are bought with a price: therefore glorify God in
your body, and in your spirit, which are God's.

1 Corinthians 6:20

Through an almost impenetrable darkness the soul seeks the purpose and reason for its existence. One day it realizes that there is a power which moves within all things and it seeks unification, not only through prayer, contemplation, and meditation, but through love. When the soul becomes a lover of the Spirit of God, it is in turn wooed by Him, wherewith He enchants the beloved with a myriad of wonders in both the inner and outer worlds. After these things have taken place, God then tests the soul to see if it is worthy to participate in the marriage feast, as were the greats before. If the tests are passed, a night of darkness envelopes the soul in the manner of a mother enveloping the fetus of her child, that it might be made ready for a coalesced state of consciousness. However, as the dark night descends, the soul enters into the great Armageddon battle which will change it from its human nature into that which is divine, or from human into an angel. Thus, human evolution is completed during this metamorphosis and a doorway to the kingdom of heaven is opened, more commonly known as the opening of the seventh seal, or the final cycle of human necessity.

In Revelation 8:1 the indwelling Christ opens the seventh seal and there is silence in heaven about the space of a half hour, a period of gestation. Time is referred to in this manner because it relates to the period between sunrise and high noon. As dawn heralds a new day and thus reiterates the beginning process of creation, high noon symbolizes the risen Christ in all his splendor. Therefore the symbol of a half hour, or half time, signifies a soul which has raised the indwelling Christ and completed unification with the spirit. It is now likened to the sun in its zenith.

After the seventh seal has been opened, John sees the seven angels, which represent the seven purifying forces of cosmic law, and they are given seven trumpets to sound the battle charge. As they raise their trumpets in a declaration of war, another angel appears before the alter which separates the soul from its immortal counterpart, and carries a golden censer of atonement. He is given much incense with which to produce a veil of smoke (symbol of ignorance and darkness) between mankind and He who sits upon the throne, thereby signifying the unworthiness of human life to look upon the glory of God until the soul has passed through the resurrection. Incense is burned to declare the day of atonement, when a flame will consume the evils of the corporeal nature and rend the veil of ignorance. This also symbolizes the fires of purification which transformed the saints who stand before the throne of God.

Thereafter the angel of judgment takes the censer, depicting the spiritual (gold) wisdom that is to descend upon the soul, and fills it with the fires of purification. The angel then casts it back upon the soul with its corporeal nature (earth), thereby causing it to perceive the wrongs it has committed during its long enticement by worldly things. At the same time, the soul, having raised the dead, is filled with great revelations and the fallacies of the flesh are shaken loose as though by a mighty earthquake.

At this point the drama becomes very exciting, for the seven purifying forces of cosmic law sound the battle cry. In that natural law is the physical expression of cosmic law, the trumpets represent the seven corresponding forces of nature. The stage is now set for the royal battle of Armageddon and the soul must walk the Via Dolorosa (the resurrection of the dead, also known as the crucifixion of the soul), for it has been found worthy to stand judgment.

Purification must be wrought not only in the body, but also in the mind and the soul before the soul can be transformed. Thus the first angel sounds a trumpet and the errors of the soul rain down upon its corporeal ways (earth) like a great hail storm and lays waste to the fertile (trees and green grass) ways of self-will. After this the second angel sounds its trumpet and the soul's self-will becomes as a great mountain which is filled with the fires of purification. After this it is cast into the sea (subconscious mind) in order to destroy the buried things which have brought disharmony within the soul through hatred, anger, jealousy, and violence.

Even now the purification of the soul is not complete, for the third angel sounds its trumpet. There falls a great star (self-will) which contains mankind's false aspiration, dreams of worldly things, impure ambitions and self pride. The star burns as a light in the dark caverns of the soul and reveals all of its past uncleanness. It might be said of this period, that the dark night is similar to wormwood, a wasteland plant which is characterized by its bitter taste. Of course, this image has been used in Revelation because it well defines the grievous plight of the soul as it stands judgment and reviews the errors of its past.

St. John of the Cross in his *Dark Night of the Soul* describes this plight of the soul in the following manner;

> *This night, which, as we say, is contemplation, produces in spiritual persons two kinds of darkness or purgation,*

corresponding to the two parts of man's nature—namely, the sensual and the spiritual. And thus the one night or purgation will be sensual, wherein the soul is purged according to sense, which is subdued to the spirit; and the other is a night of purgation which is spiritual, wherein the soul is purged and stripped according to the spirit, and subdued and made ready for the union of love with God.

Before recapitulating these scriptures, one needs to remember that the transformation of the soul is not something to be feared, but is the salvation of God which has been promised by the prophets of old. Until mankind is purified there can be no peace, either in the soul, or in the world. Neither can the soul become one with God and share in the unitive state of co-creator. The latter is worth the transformation price, for there is a sense of completion at the end of the rainbow which can never be experienced in the flesh alone. Gone are the sorrows of death, old age, and illness. Gone are the disappointments, unhappiness, loneliness, lack of self-worth, and blindness concerning the purpose of life, for the resurrection transforms all souls from mediocrity into greatness.

1. Six epochs of pre-established life progression and evolution have passed. The soul is encompassed in solitude until the indwelling Christ has been raised from the dead and shines down on the soul as the sun at high noon (1/2 hour).

1. And when he had opened the seventh seal, there was silence in heaven about the space of half an hour.

2. I looked upon the battle arena wherein the Great War would be fought within the soul. I saw the seven forces of cosmic law which emanate from the throne of God and they were given trumpets (natural law) to issue the call to battle.

2. And I saw the seven angels which stood before God; and to them were given seven trumpets.

3. Another angel stood at the doorway separating heaven and earth carrying a golden censer of atonement. Much incense was given to him that he might burn away the defilement of the soul after the manner of the saints.

3. And another angel came and stood at the altar, having a golden censer; and there was given unto him much incense, that he should offer it with the prayers of all saints upon the golden altar which was before the throne.

4. Smoke veiled the golden alter which served as a doorway between that which was mortal and that which was God.

4. And the smoke of the incense, which came with the prayers of the saints, ascended up before God out of the angel's hand.

5. And the angel took the sensor and filled it with the fires of purification, and cast it upon the soul's unwholesomeness which had been accumulated by its journey through matter. Great revelations descended upon the soul and a mighty earthquake loosened every thing hidden in the vast regions of the sub-conscious mind (bottomless pit).

5. And the angel took the censer, and filled it with fire of the altar, and cast it into the earth: and there were voices, and thunderings, and lightnings and an earthquake.

6. Then the seven powers, or cosmic laws, emanating from the throne of God, prepared to sound their trumpets (express through natural law).

6. And the seven angels which had the seven trumpets prepared themselves to sound.

7. The first angel sounded its trumpet and laid waste the pollution of the soul by purification of the great Light, causing it to turn away from its affinity for worldly things. And the enticements of the soul were burned up, as though by a great fire. (1/3 corporeal senses).

7. The first angel sounded, and there followed hail and fire mingled with blood, and they were cast upon the earth: and the third part of the trees was burnt up, and all green grass was burnt up.

8. The second angel sounded, and the mountain of self-will, which was aflame with the fires of purification, was cast into the sea (subconscious mind). The mind became a sea of blood as its indiscretions (hatred, anger, jealousy, etc.) were laid waste.

8. And the second angel sounded, and as it were a great mountain burning with fire was cast into the sea: and the third part of the sea became blood;

9. A third part of the creatures (impurities of the mind) which were in the sea were destroyed, and the third part of the ships (false ideals) were destroyed, and found no more life.[2]

9. And the third part of the creatures which were in the sea, and had life, died; and the third part of the ships were destroyed.

10. When the third angel sounded, the Light of the indwelling Christ descended from heaven, burning as a lamp, and entered the mind with its false aspirations and attachments for worldly things, and impure ambitions and self-pride.

10. And the third angel sounded, and there fell a great star from heaven, burning as it were a lamp, and it fell upon the third part of the rivers, and upon the fountain of water;

11. The name of the star is called wormwood (wasteland plant bitter to the taste) and the mind became acerbic. The soul's corporeal nature died[3] from the purification of the waters (truth) because of its past indiscretion, and its sojourn in matter were made bitter.

11. And the name of the star is called Wormwood: and the third part of the waters became wormwood; and many men died of the waters, because they were made bitter.

12. And the fourth angel sounded and the body (sun), mind (moon), and soul (stars) were isolated from the indwelling Christ and a dark night encompassed the soul and let not day or evening shine upon it.

12. And the fourth angel sounded, and the third part of the sun was smitten, and the third part of the moon, and the third part of the stars; so as the third part of them was darkened, and the day shone not for a third part of it, and the night likewise.

13. And I beheld, and heard the first angel flying through the midst of heaven, saying with a loud voice, Woe, woe, woe, to those who still contain the passions of the world, for there are yet three angels which must sound their trumpets.

13. And I beheld, and heard an angel flying through the midst of heaven, saying with a loud voice, Woe, woe, woe, to the inhabitors of the earth by reason of the other voices of the trumpet of the three angels, which are yet to sound.

CHAPTER IX

The Bottomless Pit

But if the Spirit of him that raised up Jesus from the dead
dwell in you, he that raised up Christ from the dead
shall also quicken your mortal bodies by
his Spirit that dwelleth in you.

Romans 8:11

After a wooing period between God and the soul, the indwelling Christ is raised and returns to flesh to champion the soul through the great Battle of Armageddon. This time, however, he is the possessor. At the same time the soul is shown deep and mysterious things, and has entered a chrysalis state, or a state of possession, known as the wedding chamber. This is a period of great revelation for the soul, an event that has been celebrated symbolically with much pageantry in both Judaic and Christian religions. Some of the rituals surrounding the transformation of the soul from human to divine are expressed in the Feast of the Passover (pass-over from human to divine) and Feast of the Christing (otherwise known as Christmas Dinner). .

The Christian mysteries pertaining to the resurrection of the dead are broken into four distinct categories, the *fight with Lucifer—1* (war between personal and impersonal life) and *the judg-*

ment—2 (trials to see if the soul prepared for divine transformation), *descent of spirit to live in the flesh*—3, *rebirth, and the resurrection*—4. The bottomless pit appearing in Chapter IX refers
to the freeing of the soul from its corporeal enticements. This
particular period of epigenesis generally covers the first nine years
of the resurrection. Unaccustomed to confinement by Divine will,
that aspect of the soul which is attached to matter struggles against
its imprisonment, particularly as the bottomless pit, or subconscious mind, releases a great flood of both the good and evil which
the soul has done.

Preparation begins for this exciting journey in the opening
pages of Revelation IX. The fifth angel sounds its trumpet and
the star of self-will falls from heaven. The angel is given the key to
the bottomless pit, the subconscious mind with its storehouse of
past indiscretions. As the angel opens the bottomless pit, smoke
rises out of it like the smoke of a great furnace. This refers to the
Spirit which has entered the soul to purify it of its lascivious
thoughts and deeds, thereby burning away the impurities. These
impurities, accrued through the six epochs of planetary progression, are likened to locusts descending on earth, and have great
power because they are fed by the soul's defilement (the numerous attachments and desires which continue to entice the soul to
partake of matter). They are also likened to the treacherous nature of the scorpion, whose sting carries great venom. Although
these transgressions are not allowed to hurt that which is good, as
symbolized by green grass and vegetation, they will be allowed to
cast forth their torment on the soul until it frees itself from en-
meshment in the material world, otherwise known as the five
months (body—1 bound by the four elements to matter—4).

In verses seven through eleven John describes the adversities
of the soul as an army of locusts. His description of these winged
horses (winged—ascension & horse—mind, symbolizing ascension of the mind) is similar to the image of the ancient Matichora
which had a flame colored body, a lion-like shape, three rows of

teeth, a human head and ears, blue eyes, a tail ending in a series of spikes, and a voice like the blare of trumpets. This mythological anthoropo, which ambled into medieval history, was used to symbolize mankind who was forced to sustain the weight of his spiritual nature. As the meanings of John's symbolism and the ancient mysteries are quite similar, it can be said that the impurities of the mind are like locusts aligned in ranks in preparation for battle. They wear golden crowns because they have ruled over the sensible world through human desires, and their hair is long to represent strength, while their teeth are as a lion's to ravage the mind as a carcass.

The army is arrayed in breastplates of iron, signifying inflexibility, and the sound of their wings is as the sound of many horses running to battle. This image well defines the state of the soul as the impurities of its past descend upon it. For this reason John describes the purification of the soul to be like the sting of a scorpion, and the soul must bear witness to these plagues until it is clothed in white.

There is a king over the army whose name is Abaddon, known as The Destroyer and ruler over Hades, region of the dead. As nothing new can be built until the old has been destroyed, Abaddon represents the dark aspects of the soul which bind it to the sphere of the dead, where it knew not its true self or the Light. While one woe has passed, there are yet two more to come.

The sixth angel sounded and John heard a voice speak from the golden altar which is before God. It bears four horns, signifying the four elements (the same as the four horns which adorned the Ark of the Covenant), saying, *"Loose the four elements from the great River Euphrates"* (river of life).

The remaining symbols are particularly complex. It is evident that John the Beloved was not only skilled in Hebrew symbolism, but also had a sense of humor. This becomes even more apparent in verse fifteen, as the corporeal nature (that part of the soul enmeshed in matter) is purified through the lessons invoked by its involvement with mortality (river of life/water) and the soul is purified by the Christ Light (fire) in order to ascend (air) to the throne of God. They have prepared for an hour, and a day, and a month, and a year, to slay the third part of man. Hour signifies the hour of worship when the soul and the indwelling Christ seek oneness in God. Moving on from hour to day, day signifies the seventh epoch of progression in which the soul transforms from human to divine through the resurrection of the indwelling Christ. As the remainder of the week consists of six days, six times twenty-four hours equals one hundred forty-four, the number of perfection (see Chapter 5). This is multiplied by the four cardinal points of the universe, described herein as four weeks, thereby designating philosophical rebirth, or the soul's ascension from the four elements to become one with God through the resurrection of the indwelling Christ (1 year), and destruction of the immoral aspects of the corporeal nature (l/3).

This purification of the soul will be allowed to continue for time (1), and times (2), and half time (dawn to high noon), or until the impure aspects (hatred, anger, judgment, etc.) which hold the soul in bondage to the material world have been slain and the state of union prevails, or the two become one and Christ rules resplendent as the sun at high noon.

Verses seventeen through twenty contain a description of yet another army, and although the symbolism is similar to that of the first army, there are variations worth noting. In this case, the animals carry riders wearing breastplates of fire, thereby representing warriors who purify (fire). These breastplates are comprised of the gemstone jacinth, signifying judgment, and brimstone (torment). The horses on which the riders sit have heads of lions, bodies of horses, and tails of serpents. While the horse represents the mind, as previously mentioned, the serpent is an ancient symbol of wisdom. The latter was chosen in this instance because it represents the tempter of mankind and the emblem of immortality. It also sheds its skin similar to the soul, which must discard its non spiritual nature in order to don the light-garment of the Christ body. The horses have heads of lions, representing first born, and guardian to the throne of God, who reveals the mysteries of the resurrection..

Perhaps these complex allegories can be summed up by simply stating that the powerful forces directed by the indwelling Christ will destroy all worldly enticements of the soul through wisdom and purification.

1. Then the fifth angel sounded its trumpet. The star (resurrected Christ) of Divine Will descended from heaven and was given a key to the dark regions of the subconscious (bottomless pit), which is the storehouse of the soul.

1. And the fifth angel sounded, and I saw a star fall from heaven unto the earth: and to him was given the key of the bottomless pit.

2. He opened the subconscious memories of the soul, which revealed its unlearned lessons and indiscretions—and it was burned as by a great fire. And the iniquities of the soul (physical world-sun, mind-air) rose as black smoke out of the pit.

2. And he opened the bottomless pit; and there arose a smoke out of the pit, as the smoke of a great furnace; and the sun and the air were darkened by reason of smoke of the pit.

3. And the soul bore witness to its good and its bad, and its misdeeds were as locusts laying waste to the fertile fields of past indiscretions. To them was given the power of scorpions, that by their sting they might remind the soul of those things which have kept it from reaching the Kingdom of God.

3. And there came out of the smoke locusts upon the earth: and unto them was given power, as the scorpions of the earth have power.

4. Although this grievous torment was allowed to plague the soul it was not allowed to destroy the good that dwelled therein.[1] Nor did it come upon those who had already passed into the resurrection, for they were as a temple to the living God and the bride of the lamb, and would know no more sorrow.

4. And it was commanded them that they should not hurt the grass of the earth, neither any green thing, neither any tree; but only those men which have not the seal of God on their foreheads.

5. The impurities which dwelled therein were allowed to torment the soul until it had freed itself through atonement and surrender to the indwelling Christ, or five months (soul—1, bound by the 4 elements to matter = 5). And its affliction was as the sting of a scorpion.

5. And to them it was given that they should not kill them, but that they should be tormented five months: and their torment was as the torment of a scorpion, when he striketh a man.

6. In these days the soul shall seek death and not find it; desiring to die, death shall flee from it, for the soul is an essence of God and therefore created immortal.

6. And in those days shall men seek death, and shall not find it; and shall desire to die, and death shall flee from them.

7. Then I saw the afflictions of the soul (locusts) like horses prepared for battle; and on their heads were golden crowns (wisdom) to signify rulership by Divine will to slay all human imperfections.

7. And the shapes of the locusts were like unto horses prepared unto battle; and on their heads were as it were crowns like gold, and their faces were as the faces of men.

8. These were as a woman's hair in strength and beauty, and their teeth were as the teeth of lions, that they might rend the carcass of self-will.

8. And they had hair as the hair of women, and their teeth were as the teeth of lions.

9. And they wore breastplates of iron, signifying the inflexible will of God, and the thoughts of the soul were a tumultuous like the sound of chariots (vehicles) pulled by horses (mind) running into battle.

9. And they had breastplates, as it were breastplates of iron; and the sound of their wings was as the sound of chariots of many horses running to battle.

10. And the past indiscretions of the soul stung like scorpions, and it was willed by the indwelling Christ that these should plague the soul until atonement has been rendered and the soul was freed from the enticements of worldly ways (five months—see 9:5).

10. And they had tails like unto scorpions, and there were stings in their tails: and their power was to hurt men five months.

11. Self-will ruled over the abyss of the subconscious (bottom-less pit), and he, the destroyer, known as (Abaddon), was ruler over self-will. He would lead those who had not yet entered into the resurrection of the dead into battle.

11. And they had a king over them, which is the angel of the bottomless pit, whose name in the Hebrew tongue is Abaddon, but in the Greek tongue hath his name Apollyon (god of war).

12. One woe is past; and, behold there will come two more woes (trials) hereafter.

12. One woe is past; and, behold, there some two woes more hereafter.

13. When the sixth angel sounded its trumpet, I heard the voice of the indwelling Christ speak from within the four elements of the golden altar (symbolizing the four horns of the Ark of the Covenant which stood in the room of the Holy of the Holies on which God descended to commune with Moses) before God.

13. And the sixth angel sounded, and I heard a voice from the four horns of the golden altar which is before God,

14. Saying, loose the four foundations which are bound in the great river Euphrates (signifying the flood of the mind because of its long residency on earth—four elements).[2]

14. Saying to the sixth angel which had the trumpet, Loose the four angels which are bound in the great river Euphrates.

15. And the four powers of purification were loosed (see endnote:9-2), and they were prepared to do battle until the soul completed the resurrection of the dead and slew that part of it which was bound to the corporeal world and material senses. (See chapter introduction for hour, day, month, and year.)

15. And the four angels were loosed, which were prepared for an hour, and a day, and a month, and a year, for to slay the third part of them.

16. The army signified the number of judgment (See Introduction for 200,000,00) upon the soul.

16. And the number of the army of the horsemen were two hundred thousand thousand: and I heard the number of them.

17. I saw the soul's indiscretions as horses in the vision, and they who sat on them wore breastplates of fire (purification), and of jacinth (judgment), and brimstone (desolation). They were governed by he who was first born (lions), and they inflicted mortification upon the soul that it repent of its indiscretions.[3]

17. And thus I saw the horses in the vision, and them that sat on them, having breastplates of fire, and of jacinth, and brimstone: and the heads of the horses were as the heads of lions; and out of their mouths issued fire and smoke and brimstone.

18. In time, that part of soul which inaugurated the pathway of diversification, because of its descent into matter, was destroyed through purification and desolation.

18. By these three was the third part of men killed, by the fire, and by the smoke, and by the brimstone, which issued out of their mouths.

19. And the bitterness of this knowledge laid waste to the sense enticement to worldly ways, through the exacting law of cause and effect (sting of the serpent tails).

19. For their power is in their mouth, and in their tails: for their tails were like unto serpents, and had heads, and with them they do hurt.

20. And that part of the soul's corporeal nature which had not been killed by these plagues, yet repented not over the works they had done, continued to worship the enticements of the material world and followed the path of self-will. *20. And the rest of the men which*

were not killed by these plagues yet repented not of the works of their hands, that they should not worship devils, and idols of gold, and silver, and brass, and stone, and of wood: which neither can see, nor hear, nor walk.

21. Neither had they repented of

their murders, their enchantments,[4] their promiscuity, or their thefts.
21. Neither repented they of their

murders nor of their sorceries, nor of their fornication, nor of their thefts.

CHAPTER X

Angel of the Seventh Mystery

*Let every soul be subject unto the higher powers. For there is
no power but of God: the powers that be are ordained of God.*

Romans 13:1

By this time the primary mystery of the apocalypse is
clear, and may even seem somewhat repetitious. However, it must be remembered that there are actually several battles involved. The first one takes place prior to the descent
of spirit to live in the flesh. In the Christian mysteries this period
is considered the war with Lucifer and the trial. The first, or course,
pertains to the preliminary skirmishes between that part of the
soul which is enticed by matter and that part of the soul which
seeks the state of oneness with the indwelling Christ. This will
not only determine if the soul is prepared to surrender to Divine
will, but will also create a series of tests to ascertain whether the
soul is ready to walk the Via Dolorsa (the path of the resurrection
of the dead, also known as the crucifixion of the soul). If, as previously mentioned, the soul is found to be so, the spirit descends
to live in the flesh.

Once the spirit has descended, the trumpets blow and Armageddon truly begins. The ensuing battle encompasses the

body, the mind, and the soul, and will continue until the seduction of the corporeal nature has dropped away. Thus, as
the great war continues through a series of anthropos (composite symbols representing various aspects of divine and human
transformation), it takes many forms, among them a mighty
angel from heaven clothed with a cloud and a rainbow upon
his head.

Since cloud signifies that which is not revealed, or cloaked,
the angel's shroud of clouds indicates that the truth of his mystery
is hidden and cannot be understood by the dead, or unawakened.
In Revelation 10, he still represents the indwelling Christ in mankind, for his face is as the sun, and when the sun, which is Light,
is broken down into its full spectrum it reflects the multi-colors of
the rainbow. Therefore, the Light (indwelling Christ) in man,
which is as a mighty sun, wears a rainbow for a crown and his feet
are as pillars of fire that he might descend into the world of matter
to destroy the impurities of the soul. He carries a little book which
contains all that has been, is now, and will be. This book is usually
referred to as the *Book of Life*, a history recorded in the memory
patterns of the sub-conscious mind containing the soul's journey
through life, its past, and its future as preordained in the beginning. His right foot is on the sea (subconscious mind) and the left
foot is on earth (sense enticements of the mortal world), and he
has power over the seven epochs of creative progression (seven
thunders), signifying that a part of him remains above the earth
(sea) while the other part descends to dwell on earth to purify the
soul's affinity to matter.

Naturally the soul is quite taken with itself when it perceives
the greatness resting before it, but as it partakes of the divine resurrection it finds that the deeds and thoughts of the past become
a bitter taste to the belly. As the Chapter closes, John is told that
he must go before his fellow human travelers and reveal the mystery of the resurrection of the dead, for it was to come upon all
people, tongues, nations, and rulers.

As an addendum to this chapter, it is interesting to note that the seventh angel of the seventh seal must yet sound before the mystery of God is finished. One can only assume that even greater challenges lie ahead for the soul. Yet what a glorious victory. To learn of one's destiny, the reason and purpose of life, to tame the mind, and know no separation from God, even through eternity, should be alone sufficient to fill the soul with wonder.

1. Then I saw the seventh angel descend from heaven, his mysteries hidden from those who were not awakened:[1] His face was as the sun, which expanded into a multi-colored spectrum, like a rain-bow, around his head, and his feet were as pillars of fire, for he had come to purify the soul of all indiscretion.

1. And I saw another mighty angel come down from heaven, clothed with a cloud: and a rainbow was upon his head and his face was as it were the sun, and his feet as pillars of fire.

2. In his hand he had a little book which contained the history of the soul from the beginning of creation: And he placed his right (righteous) foot upon the sea (mind) and his left foot on the earth (that part of the soul submerged in worldly enticements).

2. And he had in his hand a little book open: and he set his right foot upon the sea, and his left foot on the earth.

3. His voice was as a mighty lion protecting its domain, and his voice uttered seven thunders to herald seven more plagues which the soul had yet to endure.

3. And cried with a loud voice, as when a lion roareth: and when he had cried, seven thunders uttered their voices.

4. When the seven angels of the seven seals had sounded, I began to write. I heard the voice of the resurrected Christ say to me, "Seal these things which have been revealed to you and do not write them."

4. And when the seven thunders had uttered their voices, I was about to write: and I heard a voice from heaven saying unto me, Seal up those things which the seven thunders uttered, and write them not.

5. Then he, who ruled the mind and corporeal nature of the soul, raised his hand to heaven (right hand).

6. And swore by God who has lived forever and created heaven and earth, and all things therein, that there would be no more time for mankind.

7. That during the final phase of the soul progression the mystery of God would be finished, as it had been prophesied by all prophets since the beginning.

8. The voice which I heard from heaven spoke to me again saying, "Go and take the book which has been written by the deeds and thoughts of the soul during its sojourn into matter, and which has now been opened by the indwelling Christ.

9. I went to him, requesting, "Give me the book of life." And he replied, "Take it, and consume the knowledge therein, for it reveals all that the soul has experienced, what has been and is, although it will be abominable to you. Even so, it contains the future which shall be sweet as honey in your mouth."

5. And the angel which I saw stand upon the sea and upon the earth lifted up his hand to heaven.

6. And sware by him that liveth for ever and ever, who created heaven, and the things that therein are, and the earth, and the things that threin are, and the sea, and the things which are therein, that there should be time no longer.

7. But in the days of the voice of the seventh angel, when he shall begin to sound, the mystery of God should be finished, as he hath declared to his servants the prophets.

8. And the voice which I heard from heaven spake unto me again, and said, Go and take the little book which is open in the hand of the angel which standeth upon the sea and upon the earth.

9. And I went unto the angel, and said unto him, Give me the little book. And he said unto me, Take it, and eat it up; and it shall make thy belly bitter, but it shall be in thy mouth sweet as honey.

10. Then I took the book and consumed it (viewed all that a soul has encountered through its journey through matter), and that which was yet to be was sweet to my taste. Then I saw that which is and had been and it was loathsome to me, for I saw those who were unawakened imprisoned by wars and hatred, and their souls, which were of God, knew no light.

11. And he said to me, "You must prophesy, for this knowledge which has been given to you must now be revealed to all nations and peoples."

10. And I took the little book out of the angel's hand, and ate it up; and it was in my mouth sweet as honey: and as soon as I had eaten it, my belly was bitter.

11. And he said unto me, Thou must prophesy again before many peoples, and nations, and tongues, and kings.

The path to immortality is hard, and only a few find it.
The rest await the Great day when the wheels of the
universe shall be stopped and the immortal sparks
shall escape from the sheaths of substance.
Woe unto those who wait, for they must return again
unconscious and unknowing, to the seed—ground of stars,
and await a new beginning. Those who are
saved by the light of the mystery which I have revealed
unto you O Hermes, and which I now bid you to establish
among men, shall return again to the Father who
dwelleth in the White Light, and they shall become
powers in God. This is the way of Good and is revealed
only to them that have wisdom ... I order you to
go forth, to become as a guide to those
who wander in darkness.

The Divine Pymander,
translated from Arabic and Greek
by Dr. Everard (1650)

CHAPTER XI

The Two Witnesses

*And I will pray to the Father, and he shall give you another
Comforter, that he may abide with you forever; Even the
Spirit of truth; whom the world cannot receive, because
it seeth him not, neither knoweth him: but ye know
him; for he dwelleth with you, and shall be in you.*

St. John 14:16-17

Again John the Beloved has skillfully hidden the mysteries of the resurrection in an allegory of numbers. For
the most part the modern world is unaware of the ancient mysteries disclosing those things which are revealed through
a contemplative mind. While it has been the common practice of
mystics (a person who experiences mystical union or direct communion with God) throughout the ages to study the outer world
of matter in order to comprehend the inner secrets of the soul, a
treasure chest of hidden symbolism is buried amid the ancient
Christian writings and scriptures, as well as Hebrew mysticism.
The latter, with its numerical keys, is based upon the Egyptian
and Hebrew mysteries, and contains important clues to unravel-

ing the mysteries of Moses as well as the Apocalypse. One such example takes place in Revelation 11, for the temple and its court is based upon Moses' tabernacle in the wilderness as outlined in Exodus, the twenty-fifth chapter.

In Revelation 11:1 John is given a measuring reed (an ancient unit of measure equaling six times a cubit plus six handbreadths—Ezekiel 40:5) to measure those bound to the sixth epoch of soul progression to see if they are ready to enter into marriage with the lamb. Next he is told not to evaluate those who have not yet entered, for they must wander until they have freed themselves from imprisonment to matter (4 elements) and united the soul with the indwelling Christ (2).

Following these measurements, power is given to two witnesses, one the indwelling Christ, and the other the soul, both of which must attend the passage of the soul's complete transformation for two thousand two hundred and three score days. These numbers reflect the union of the soul to its divine counterpart (2) through the amalgamation of the body, mind and soul (3). As these two natures are the heart of mysteries, particularly in religion and philosophy, they also describe the two olive trees and two candlesticks which stand before God.

It is said that if anyone who seeks to hurt the soul or the indwelling Christ, words of great truth will proceed out of their holy mouths and destroy the ignorance of their enemies. In other words, the precise law of cause and effect will prevail, and he who kills shall also be killed through transfiguration. Power is given to the two witnesses to close the corporeal nature away from any semblance of heavenly estate, turn the mind to blood, and plague the physical counterpart until its malevolent aspects have been destroyed. When the soul's review of that which has been, is, and will be, has been completed, a great beast rises out of the deep regions of the subconscious to make war against them and shall kill them, or at least give the appearance that they have been killed (see 11:7-9).

This mount of transformation can be more clearly explained through the actual psychological process which occurs in this particular phase of the soul's enticement by the indwelling Christ. Once God has endowed the soul by descending to live in the flesh, causing a wellspring of knowledge to pour out in form of great mystical revelations, as well as revealing the misnomers of the soul, the soul enters into the dark night. As it, and its divine counterpart, reach this state of seeming death, the lesser nature which consists of self-will, ignorance, hatred, anger, intolerance and obsession with the material world, rises out of the deep abyss to fight against the heavenly state which is imposing Divine will. Therefore, all emotions, feelings and mental states are intensified during the apocalyptic battle, leaving that aspect of the soul bound to matter with a sense that all divinity has fled from it and will never be experienced again. This state will prevail until the marriage of the lamb has taken place and the indwelling Christ rules supreme.

John the Beloved compares this remarkable estate with the city of Sodom and the country of Egypt, in that both were examples of the iniquitous ways of mankind. Sodom, once full of tar pits, salt, and free sulfur, was destroyed during the twenty-first century BC. by fire as a result of a great earthquake which caused a cataclysmic explosion. Carried up into the air, the hot ploding salt and sulfur literally caused a rain of fire and brimstone over the whole plain. It was believed that the city was destroyed by God as a result of its great wickedness.

Little more can be said about Egypt, once a land of great power and wealth. Constantly besieged by war until its original essence began to decline after Rameses III repulsed the invading Sea People (including the Philistines), its decline was blamed upon the barbaric nature of people who were greedy and desirous of personal gain. Therefore John's reference to Sodom and Egypt represents that aspect of the soul which is bound to the temporal world of desires and self-will, for it is that part of the corporeal nature which

brings death and destruction. Although specters of past degrada-
tion dance in the streets of the conscience and mind, they cannot
bury that part of the soul which is in harmony with the indwelling Christ. In time these evils of human nature, in the form of the
ego, will rise against that which is holy and be destroyed. Thus, in
that same hour there is a great shaking loose, and the body, mind and
soul, must overcome its weaknesses through atonement with God.

Finally, the seventh angel of the seventh seal sounds its horn
and a proclamation is made that the kingdoms of this world have
become the kingdoms of God and of the indwelling Christ; and
that He should reign forever and ever. The temple of the soul is
opened to heaven after this and the mystery of the ark of the
covenant is revealed amid great inner revelations, which is likened
to thunderings (heralding), earthquakes (shaking loose), and great
hail (descending petulance).

The summation of these adventures which descend upon the
soul is eloquently written in an excerpt from the Divine Pymander:

> *Because the Father of all things consists of Life and
> Light, whereof man is made. If therefore, a man shall learn
> and understand the nature of Life and Light, then shall he
> pass into the eternal Life and Light. (Light) will not permit
> the evil senses to control the body of those who love (him),
> nor will (he) allow evil emotions and evil thoughts to enter
> them. (He) becomes a porter or doorkeeper and shuts out
> evil, protecting the wise from their own lower nature. But
> to the wicked, the envious and the covetous, (he) come(s)
> not, for such cannot understand the mysteries of the Mind;
> therefore (he is) unwelcome. (He) leave(s) them to the
> avenging demon that they are making in their own souls,
> for each evil each day increases itself and torments man
> more sharply, and each evil deed adds to the evil deeds that
> are gone before until finally evil destroys itself. The punish-
> ment of desire is the agony of fulfillment."*

1. I was given a measuring reed[1] and the angel stood, saying, "Judge those who have built the inner temple for God, the altar which serves as bridge between the terrestrial celestial worlds, and those who have entered into the resurrection, that they might be evaluated according to their deeds

1. And there was given me a reed like unto a rod: and the angel stood, saying, Rise, and measure the temple of God, and the altar, and them that worship therein.

2. "Do not measure the court (body) without, wherein dwell those who have not entered into marriage with the lamb. These cannot enter into the kingdom of God (holy city) until they have raised the soul from its imprisonment to the corporeal world (bondage to matter by the four elements—40) and resurrected the indwelling Christ (soul-1/spirit 1=2).

2. But the court which is without the temple leave out, and measure it not; for it is given unto the Gentiles: and the holy city shall they tread under foot forty and two months.

3. "I will give power to the indwelling Christ, and the soul (2 witnesses), that they bear witness to all which has been, is, and will be. By his descent into matter, he shall champion the soul through darkness and purgation (clothed in sackcloth) until the soul, the inner Christ and God are one (1-000) through the soul's union with the Lamb (2-00) and the resurrection of the dead is completed (10-10-10=three score).

3. And I will give power unto my two witnesses, and they shall prophesy a thousand two hundred and three-score days, clothed in sackcloth.

4. "These are also the two olive trees and the two candlesticks, which through their union are now one in God (standing before God) on earth.

4. These are the two olive trees, and two candle sticks standing before the God of the earth.

5. "And transgressions born of temporal matter must not rise up against the soul and the indwelling Christ, or they shall reap what they have sown and be destroyed in the fires of purification.

5. And if any man will hurt them, fire proceedeth out of their mouth, and devoureth their enemies: and if any man will hurt them, he must in this manner be killed.

6. "The indwelling Christ has power to shut heaven away from the corporeal nature, that it become as a desert without rain and a mind beset by the indiscretions of its past. And these witnesses are given power to smite the nefarious aspects of this lower nature (ego-dragon) until atonement has been completed.

6. These have power to shut heaven, that it rain not in the days of their prophecy: and have power over waters to turn them to blood, and to smite the earth with all plagues, as often as they will.

7. "And when they have finished their evidence, that which is less in the soul (ego-dragon) shall rise out of the deep abyss of the subconscious and make war against that which is holy and true. And for a time no light shall enter into soul. (ref: *Dark Night of Soul,* St. John of the Cross)[2].

7. And when they shall have finished their testimony, the beast that ascendeth out of the bottomless pit shall make war against them, and shall overcome them, and kill them.

8. "They shall be submerged by the indiscretions which were wrought by the soul's journey through matter. And there shall be no more peace in the body or in the mind because these imprisoned that which was divine.

8. And their dead bodies shall lie in the street of the great city, which spiritually is called Sodom and Egypt, where also our Lord was crucified.

9. "And the worldly aspects of the soul shall be separated from its heavenly estate until it has atoned for its evils and become one with its divine counterpart (1-2 = 3 days), and the sovereignty of the indwelling Christ is with out end (half day, or as the light at high noon).

9. And they of the people and kindreds and tongues and nations shall see their dead bodies three days and an half, and shall not suffer their dead bodies to be put in graves.

10. "The soul will fall into great tribulation, for its counterfeiting ways shall seek to draw it back into the enticements of the world, which is now without Light."

10. And they that dwell upon the earth shall rejoice over them, and make merry, and shall send gifts one to another; because these two prophets tormented them that dwelt on the earth.

11. Following the submission of the body, mind, and soul, and when the indwelling Christ is resplendent in the soul as the sun is resplendent in the heavens at high noon, judgment shall be rendered against all which is inferior. The worldly nature of the soul shall fear these reprisals greatly because of its imprudent transgressions.

11. And after three days and a half the Spirit of life from God entered into them, and they stood upon their feet; and great fear fell upon them which saw them.

12. And the voice of God called forth his Son, the indwelling Christ, and his Son's consort, the soul, and they ascended to heaven (oneness with God), their divine estate separated (cloud-hidden) from that part of the soul still attracted to worldly things.

12. And they heard a great voice from heaven saying unto them, Come up thither. And they ascended up to heaven in a cloud; and their enemies beheld them.

13. And in the twelfth hour (when the two become one) there was a great earthquake within the soul as it surrendered to Divine will (1-0) and entered into the resurrection of the dead (7-000—7th epoch, or final phase of human progression). And those enticements of the mind which were of the world caused the mind to become affrighted and it sought purification.

13. And the same hour was there a great earthquake, and the tenth part of the city fell, and in the earthquake were slain of men seven thousand: and the remnant were affrighted, and gave glory to the God of heaven.

14. And the second woe (purification of the mind) is past; and behold the third woe (purification of the soul), comes quickly.

14. The second woe is past; and, behold, the third woe cometh quickly.

15. After these things were shown, I beheld the seventh angel sound its trumpet and the voice of God spoke, saying, "The kingdoms of the world have now become the kingdoms of God, and the indwelling Christ shall reign forever and ever."[3]

15. And the seventh angel sounded; and there were great voices in heaven, saying, The kingdoms of this world are become the kingdoms of our Lord, and of his Christ; and he shall reign forever and ever.

16. And the soul, which had been imprisoned by the four elements to the material world, having raised the indwelling Christ (2-4) surrendered to Divine will. (see 4:4)

16. And the four and twenty elders, which sat before God on their seats, fell upon their faces, and worshipped God.

17. Saying, " We give thanks, O Lord God Almighty, which is, which has been since the beginning, and which is yet to come; because you are all powerful and have reigned forever."

17. Saying, We give thee thanks, O Lord God Almighty, which art, and wast, and art to come; because thou hast taken to thee thy great power, and hast reigned.

18. And every soul bound to worldly desires and aspirations, who has not yet entered into the resurrection, is angry that your wrath is come. They know that they shall be judged as your servants, prophets, saints, and those that fear your name, both small and great, have been judged; and that you will destroy all within them which lay waste to the earth.

18. And the nations were angry, and thy wrath is come, and the time of the dead, that they should be judged, and that thou shouldst give reward unto thy servants the prophets, and to the saints, and them that fear thy name, small and great; and shouldst destroy them which destroy the earth.

19. Then, the temple within all souls was opened and the divine plan of God revealed: and there were revelations (lightnings), and a mighty upheaval within the soul. The fields of the past were laid barren as though by a great hail.

19. And the temple of God was opened in heaven, and there was seen in his temple the ark of his testament: and there were lightnings, and voices, and thunderings, and an earthquake, and great hail.

SECTION II

THE BATTLE
OF ARMAGEDDON

*Purification
of the Soul*

Fall of the Dragon

*He that rejecteth me, and receiveth not my words, hath
one that judgeth him: the words that I have spoken,
the same shall judge him in the last day.*

St. John 12:48

During the period following Jesus' death on the cross the apostles not only wove the great mystical traditions of antiquity into fire and brimstone, but created mighty anthropos in the form of dragons and colorful beasts to guard the great secrets of the Apocalypse (process of transformation from human to divine). In chapters twelve and thirteen these creatures begin to take on life and assume the disguise of St. John's greatest villains. The symbolism is massive and the battle climactic, but all of this proclaims the most intriguing section of the entire Apocalypse.

St. Cyril of Alexandria (AD. 412) even wrote in the Seventh Book of Julian:

*These Mysteries are so profound and so exalted, that they
can be comprehended only by those who are enlightened. I
should say much more, if I were not afraid of being heard*

111

*by those who are not initiated; because men are apt to
deride what they do not understand. And the ignorant not
being aware of the weakness of their minds, condemn what
they ought most to venerate.*

Sixteen hundred years have passed since St. Cyril wrote these words. Now it is the twenty-first century and mankind has escaped earth's gravity field to soar in outer space amid the stars, and his intellect has been greatly influenced under the guiding hand of academia. The human race has discovered the *Grand Unified Theory,* and has risen to noble greatness in the fields of religion, philosophy and science. Perhaps it is possible at last to rent the masks of St. John's beasts and dragons, and leave the creatures to perish in the magnificent descent of the New Jerusalem.

The symbolism will not be quite so bewildering if one remembers that the first dragon and two subsequent beasts signify the purification of the body, mind, and soul.

Chapter 12 opens with a woman, commonly referred to as the mother of the mysteries, and a dragon with seven heads, signifying the seven epochs of progressive creation which have heretofore been ruled over by the corporeal senses. The mother of the mysteries represents that aspect of the soul which will give birth to the indwelling Christ. This symbol originally appeared in Egyptian traditions as Isis, the virgin of the world, and later under other names as the first principle of natural femininity.

This adversary of the mother of divine birth is none other than a wily old dragon, known as the ego or self-will. In the ancient mysteries he was called Typhon meaning insolence and pride, for egotism, self-centeredness, and pride are the deadly enemies of divine transformation. The dragon is red, to import the sacrifice of the indwelling Christ who accepted imprisonment in the world of matter to assure the continued divinity of the soul. He also possesses ten horns and seven crowns, thereby reflecting matter's domination over that which is holy throughout the seven

(7) cycles of progressive necessity (epochs), after which the soul reaches oneness with God (1-0).

The dragon (ego & self-will) is ferocious and draws that aspect of the soul which is celestial into the world of matter, and prepares to devour the indwelling Christ child which is being raised from the womb of the soul's spiritual nature. The woman brings forth the indwelling Christ child who will ultimately rule all nations with inflexible will (iron) amid the chaos of worldly ways. The indwelling Christ, however, freed from the imprisonment of human will, rises to oneness with God, leaving its divine counterpart in desolation. This is necessary, for the soul must face purgation of its past in order to be sanctified for its marriage to the lamb.

After these things have come to pass, God, and the Son of God, which is now risen from the dead, prepares to administer the forces of purification upon the subconscious aspects of the soul which contains many impurities from its long journey through matter. These will continue to fight against the soul until it has united with the indwelling Christ and freed itself from the enticements of mortality (1,260).

The great war of Armageddon begins; Michael,[1] the personification of the heavenly protector, descends with his forces of purification to attack the ego (self-will) which harbors hatred, anger, weakness, condemnation and war, and these things are cast out of the soul through purgation and transmutation. In this particular instance John refers to this lower nature in humanity as the Devil, or Satan, previously clarified as a Christian anthropose representing the sinister side of human life. In that darkness cannot defeat light, that part of the soul which has enmeshed itself in the material world and thereby deceived itself because it had no knowledge of its divine estate, is isolated to undergo transmutation.

A loud voice in heaven speaks, saying that the time has come for the salvation of God and His kingdom, and for the power of his Son. The ego's self-centeredness (Satan, the dragon) has been cast down through the sacrifice and resurrection of the indwelling Christ, and by the Law (testimony) which is inherent in the nature of all people. That part of the soul which is in a divine estate rejoices over the transfiguration which it is undergoing, but that part enmeshed in the corporeal sense world suffers greatly when the impurities of the mind (sea) and body (earth) fall upon it in great wrath.

As the erroneous ways of the past are brought into conscious awareness, the soul suffers great upheaval. It is given the knowledge and wisdom, however, to ascend out of the wilderness and become united with its divine counterpart (one in God), after which the indwelling Christ rules without end. Although the vast subconscious sea (subconscious mind) has let loose a flood of transgressions, the soul's utilization of natural law to purify the body is imperative. In that the body is a temple of the living God (I Corinthians 3:16), it must be purified of its defilement, for that which is not in harmony with natural law brings distemper, illness, and death. Because of this, the body draws corresponding negative forces which strengthen the dragon.

Chapter XII closes with the royal battle in full progress, as the self-will finds it very difficult to surrender to the will of God and to live under the absolute possessive control of the indwelling Christ.

For now, amid throes of death, new life is coming to birth,
and the pangs of travail set in,
as at last there enters the world the man-child long conceived.
And when he comes to birth, all those pangs of travail
that rack the world's
great womb – that crucible of conception –
will take a sudden turn; what
has been conceived with all the bale of a viper will end
at the moment of birth.

Dead Sea Scrolls, The Book of Hymns, III,10-15, Gaster

1. I beheld a great wonder in heaven (state of consciousness) as the divine mother principle (wisdom) of the indwelling Christ came forth clothed with the sun (body), and the moon under her feet (wisdom would reign over the mind). Through divine birth the soul and her Son would unite and rule over the worldly nature and its aspirations forever (1-2 stars).

1. And there appeared a great wonder in heaven; a woman clothed with the sun, and moon under her feet, and upon her head a crown of twelve stars.

2. And the mother of wisdom was pregnant with the Christ child and travailing in birth and pained to be delivered (the struggle of the soul to resurrect the indwelling Christ).

2. And she being with child cried, travailing in birth, and pained to be delivered.

3. Then, there appeared another wonder in heaven and I beheld a great red (bloodshed and sacrifice) dragon (ego and self-will), and he had seven heads (7 epochs of earth progression through matter) and bearing seven crowns (ego & self-will's rulership over the 7 phases of soul progression). And he had ten horns, for he would continue to rule until the indwelling Christ and soul became one (1-0).

3. And there appeared another wonder in heaven; and behold a great red dragon, having seven heads and ten horns, and seven crowns upon his head.

4. The iniquities dwelling in the subconscious region (bottomless pit) of the soul because of the soul's journey through matter were revealed, and that part of the soul wherein resided ego & self-will (dragon) sought to destroy the child being born from the divine mother of wisdom (self-will vs. divine-will).

4. And his tail drew the third part of the stars of heaven, and did cast them to the earth: and the dragon stood before the woman which was ready to be delivered, for to devour her child as soon as it was born.

5. And she brought forth the indwelling Christ who was to rule all nations with inflexible will (rod of iron); and he was raised into the immortal regions of the soul wherein stands the throne of God and He who abides therein.

5. And she brought forth a man child who was to rule all nations with a rod of iron: and her child was caught up unto God, and to his throne.

6. And the mother of wisdom entered into isolation as ordained by God, where she would be taught in the ways of heaven until the soul was cleansed and prepared for the holy marriage to its divine counterpart—through the union of the body, mind and soul (1,260)²

6. And the woman fled into the wilderness, where she hath a place prepared of God, that they should feed her there a thousand two hundred and three-score days.

7. A great war was wrought within the soul as the forces of Light fought against the dragon (ego and self-will) and his angels (hatred—anger—jealousy—etc.)

7. And there was a war in heaven: Michael and his angels fought against the dragon; and the dragon fought and his angels.

8. Evil prevailed not; neither could its way remain a part of that which was holy.

8. And prevailed not; neither was their place found any more in heaven.

9. And the ego which had deceived the soul with its enticements was cast out, and the dark angels of hatred, anger, lust, gluttony, slothfulness, ignorance and superstition were cast out with it.

9. And the great dragon was cast out, that old serpent, called the Devil, and Satan, which deceiveth the whole world: he was cast out into the earth, and angels were cast out with him.

10. Then I heard that, which was holy, saying, "The time has come for the salvation of the soul, and for the will of God and the power of the Indwelling Christ to rule: for the prince of darkness and ignorance which has tormented those of Light (brethren) is cast down.

10. And I heard a loud voice saying in heaven, Now is come salvation and strength, and the kingdom of our God, and the power of his Christ: for the accuser of our brethren is cast down, which accused them before God day and night.

11. Those who had entered into the resurrection overcame ego and self-will through the resurrection of the indwelling Christ. They no longer loved the vagrancies of the world, but worked for the common good of all people until death of the physical body.[3]

11. And they overcame him by the blood of the Lamb, and by the word of their testimony; and they loved not their lives unto the death.

12. Therefore rejoice, you who have raised the inner Christ and dwell in heaven. Woe to those who remain bound by the chains of the body and the mind. For the ego and self-will (devil) has come upon you in great wrath, because it has but a short time remaining.

12. Therefore rejoice, ye heavens, and ye that dwell in them. Woe to the inhabitors of the earth and of the sea! For the devil is come down unto you, having great wrath, because he knoweth that he hath but a short time.

13. And those indiscretions buried in the subconscious aspect of the soul persecuted it (war between the personal and impersonal life, or human vs. divine), which had given birth to the indwelling Christ.

13. When the dragon saw that he was cast unto the earth, he persecuted the woman which brought forth the man child.

14. And the soul was raised like a great eagle that it might enter the regions between the mortal and immortal (wilderness and desolation). There she was nourished by great revelations, until she had been purified and entered into the holy marriages (time—1, times—2, 1/2—time, as the sun at high noon).

14. And to the woman were given two wings of a great eagle, that she might fly into the wilderness, into her place, where she is nourished for a time, and times, and half a time, from the face of the serpent.

15. The dragon (ego and self-will) let loose a flood of past iniquities within the soul, that it might feel unworthy to enter the kingdom of heaven.

15. And the serpent cast out of his mouth water as a flood after the woman, that he might cause her to be carried away in the flood.

16. And the soul's compliance with the laws of nature (earth-body purification), however, helped the soul, and as the body was made pure the soul's defilement was transformed.

16. And the earth helped the woman and earth opened her mouth, and swallowed up the flood which the dragon cast out of his mouth.

17. The dragon (ego and self-will) was wroth over the revelations of its transgressions and went forth to make war upon the indwelling Christ, who commanded the forces of cosmic law and championed the redemption of the soul.

17. And the dragon was wroth with the woman, and went to make war with the remnant of her seed, which keep the commandments of God, and have the testimony of Jesus Christ.

CHAPTER XIII

Beasts of the Sea

*Whereby, when ye read, ye may understand my knowledge in
the mystery of Christ, Which in other ages was not made
known unto the sons of men, as it is now revealed unto
his holy apostles and prophets by the Spirit;*

Ephesians 3:4-5

s the battle of Armageddon continues and the soul has
been inundated by its own injustices which emanate
from the great reservoir of the subconscious, it faces
yet more challenges. These are the beasts of the mind and the
body. The first dragon, which depicts the lower nature, or the ego
and self-will (also referred to as Satan, or the anti-Christ), is now
cast down from his sovereignty. This means the soul no longer
believes itself to be simply a mortal being. Having raised the indwelling Christ from the very depth of its spiritual womb, it now
knows that the path of self-will has led it out of the Garden of
Eden into the darkness of matter (cast out of heaven). Identifying
itself with matter, it believed that life was temporal and therefore,
to a certain extent, followed a path of sense gratification, first in-
stinctive and later through matter's enticements which established
desires. This built a large accumulation of indiscretions which were

in direct violation of the forward movement of cosmic order (God's divine plan).

That aspect of the soul enmeshed in a corporeal nature with its ego & self-will (dragon) is comprised of the physical body, feelings, emotions, conscious mind, and the semi-material, subtle sheath, which circumscribes all of the forgoing. Quite naturally, the *dragon* has been appointed guardian of the lesser aspects of the soul because it contains the residual of the soul's unlearned lessons. In thinking about this peculiar phenomenon one is reminded of the famous story depicting Adam's return to the Garden of Eden: (Adam-collective man, referring to the intellect's descent into homogeneal ground) Hebraic Tongue II:19-25, d'Olivet)

> *Soon after Adam's return to the Garden of Eden he came upon a great dragon wrapped around the Tree of Knowledge, or the Tree of Life, and the dragon asked, "Do you recognize me, Adam?" Adam replied, "Yes, you are Satan who led me astray."*
>
> *The dragon threshed its tail and replied, "Indeed I am Satan, guardian of the Tree of Knowledge, and I have vowed that none whom I can lead astray shall partake of its fruits. I have turned you against the illusion of worldliness and weaned you of desire. I am your adversary, the one who pleads your destruction before the Eternal Tribunal."*

In that the spirit is perfect, the great conflict occurs in the hidden layers of the soul, engulfing the mind, and compelling the soul to review its indiscretions. The mind subsequently courses through the body and causes it to act. It might be said, therefore, that one who journeys into the New Jerusalem must raise the indwelling Christ by casting the ego & self-will (dragon) out of its mortal nature, battle the patterns of impure thoughts (first beast), and finally rise beyond the temptations of the flesh (second beast) which reflect, or exercise, the powers of the first beast, i.e., desires and aspirations which feed the mind.

As Revelation 13 ends, the next phase of the war, those human aspects of the soul (lower) nature, which has deceived the soul into believing it is only mortal, is healed of its deadly wound, the ego. Now it rises angrily to make war on those who no longer follow the way of self-will and kills them. This does not mean death to the physical body, but that those who have entered into the resurrection of the dead are no longer bound by the passions and the temptations of matter. Those who do worship the beast, or continue on the path of human obsession, bear the mark of the beast, or his name, or the number of his name. The number of his name is the number of man, which is six hundred sixty-six (666), meaning body, soul and spirit are, or have been, bound to the sixth epoch of necessary evolution (human life). Obviously the mark is black to indicate darkness and ignorance, and his name is Satan, ruler of the underworld, meaning ego & self-will rules over mortality.

1. I, John, stood upon the sand (that part of the soul bound to the corporeal senses), and I saw a great beast rise up out of the sea (subconscious mind), which had seven heads signifying the seven epochs of progressive necessity. His head bore ten horns and ten crowns (see XII:3), for he would rule over the senses until the soul completed judgment. He contained the collective indiscretions of the soul (blasphemy).

1. And I stood upon the sand of the sea, and saw a beast rise up out of the sea, having seven heads and ten horns, and upon his horns ten crowns, and upon his heads the name of blasphemy.

2. The beast which I saw was like a leopard (black spots—treachery and cunning). His feet had the power of the bear, and his mouth was as a mighty lion that he might rend the soul as a carcass.[1] And the dragon (ego) gave him his power.

2. And the beast which I was like unto a leopard, and his feet were as the feet of a bear, and his mouth as the mouth of a lion: and dragon gave him his power, and his seat, and great authority.

3. I saw one of his heads (the primary ego) had been wounded to death by the soul's resurrection of the indwelling Christ. His deadly wound was healed, however, as the worldly nature of the soul sought to return to the familiarity of the past, even as the world follows deceit and destruction.

3. And I saw one of his heads as it were wounded to death; and his deadly wound was healed: and all the world wondered after the beast.

4. And those who were yet bound to the senses worshipped the ways of ego and self-will (dragon) which gave power to the beast (mind): And they worshipped those things which sustained the corruptness of the mind, saying, "What people are like the beast? Who is powerful enough to make war against him?"

4. And they worshipped the dragon which gave power unto the beast: and they worshipped the beast, saying, Who is like unto the beast? Who is able to make war with him?

5. And power was given to subconscious to reveal the improprieties of the soul until the soul had purified and atoned for her indiscretions through the resurrection of indwelling Christ, which has been raised from his bondage by the four elements (4-0)—thereby uniting the soul and her divine counterpart (2).

5. And there was given unto him a mouth speaking great things and blasphemies; and power was given unto him to continue forty and two months.

6. And the subconscious released a flood of iniquities (harm done to others and the wayward actions wrought through ignorance), which had debased God, his name, his tabernacle (soul), and those who had already passed into the resurrection of the dead.

6. And he opened his mouth in blasphemy against God, to blaspheme his name, and his tabernacle, and them that dwell in heaven.

7. Divine-will gave the beast power to make war against that which was holy, and seek to overcome, that the soul become strong and pure. He is known as the tempter of worldly enticements and lives in all kindred, tongues, and nations.

7. And it was given unto him to make war with the saints, and to overcome them: and power was given him over all kindreds, and tongues, and nations.

8. Those who remained bound to the world of matter and the material senses followed the path of worldly ways, as they had yet to raise the indwelling Christ—who had descended to live in the soul's unknowingness at the inception of the world.

8. And all that dwell upon the earth shall worship him, whose names are not written in the book of life of the Lamb slain from the foundation of the world.

9. If any man understand these mysteries, let him hear.

9. If any man have an ear, let him hear.

10. Every soul must reap that which it has sown. Therefore, whosoever shall lead into captivity shall also be imprisoned; and whosoever kills must be killed, for purification and obedience to the ways of heaven are the rewards of saints.

10. He that leadeth into captivity shall go into captivity: he that killeth with a sword must be killed with the sword. Here is the patience and the faith of the saints.

11. I beheld another beast coming out of soul, filled with worldly desires and false aspirations (1st beast—impure thoughts. 2nd beast—temptations of the flesh. See: XIII Intro. p:3) He had two horns (one horn to symbolize the indwelling Christ and one horn to symbolize the soul) like a lamb and he set forth to entice the soul to continue its worldly ways (spake like a dragon).[2]

11. And I beheld another beast coming up out of the earth; and he had two horns like a lamb, and he spake as dragon.

12. And he signified the soul's bondage to ego and self-will, and sought to lead the soul to follow the ways of self-will, which had received a mortal blow when the soul entered into the resurrection. Now his power was again strengthened by the desires of the soul.

12. And he exerciseth all the power of the first beast before him, and causeth the earth and them which dwell therein to worship the first beast, whose deadly wound was healed.

13. He did great wonders, for he was built of material wealth, worldly powers, fame and glorification of worldly things. And he caused great tribulation to fall upon the soul (human desires vs. Divine will).

13. And he doeth great wonders, so that he maketh fire come down from heaven on the earth in the sight of men.

14. Those who were bound by the chains of human ignorance were deceived by worldly ways; and they built their aspirations on the ways of flesh and self-will.

14. And deceiveth them that dwell on the earth by the means of those miracles which he had power to do in the sight of the beast; saying to them that dwell on earth, that they should make an image to the beast, which had the wound by a sword and and did live.

15. The ways of earth were powerful upon the soul, but seeing its indiscretions it prepares to turn away from its false values and come unto the marriage with the lamb (ego and self-will surrenders to divine will, thereby killed of its worldly ways).

15. And he had power to give life unto the image of the beast, that the image of the beast should both speak, and cause that as many as would not worship the image of the beast should be killed.

16. Then he caused all, both small and great, rich and poor, free and bond, who followed in the ways of the world, to receive a mark (black) in their right hand (indicating opposition to righteousness), or in their forehead (darkness, ignorance and unknowing).

16. And he causeth all, both small and great, rich and poor, free and bond, to receive a mark in their right hand, or in their foreheads.

17. And only those who had not entered into the resurrection, and walked in darkness and ignorance continued to follow the path of worldly enticement.

17. And that no man might buy or sell, save he that had the mark, or the name of the beast, or the number of his name.

18. Let those who understand these mysteries count the number of the beast, for it is 600-60-6, *the number of man* whose body, mind and soul are enmeshed in the sixth evolutionary epoch of earth's progression. (666 - human life). See Genesis 1:27:31.

18. Here is wisdom. Let him that hath understanding count the number of the beast: for it is the number of a man; and his number is Six hundred threescore and six.

The Reapers

*But when it pleased God, who separated me from my
mother's womb, and called me by his grace, To reveal his
Son in me, that I might preach him among the heathen;
immediately I conferred not with flesh and blood.*

Galations 1:15-16

As the magnificent odyssey of the soul continues to un-
ravel from the illusive threads of mystery and intrigue, the
indwelling Christ appears on Mount Sion with those who
have completed the resurrection of the dead. John the Beloved uses
the term Mount Sion to symbolize the lofty place within the soul
where dwells the risen Christ. The opening can be looked upon
either singularly or collectively, for by now the number one hundred forty-four thousand (see 7:4) is recognized as a state of consciousness rather than a quantity. Collectively, this signifies a time
when all mortals will enter into the resurrection and fulfill the
great prophesy of the coming messiah. Although Jesus, who became known as the Christ, well represented this prophesy on earth,
the people of antiquity did not realize that the long-awaited deliv-
erer would actually be born within them during the final, or seventh, epoch of evolutionary progression.

As John again enters that state of Cosmic Consciousness (oneness with the mind of God), wherein the great mysteries are being revealed, he sees those who have been transformed by the risen Christ. They bear the name of God upon their forehead, which is Yahweh, or Jehovah, meaning Lord. Standing before the throne they sing a new song, for they are no longer bound by the material senses and have come to see through the fascination of temporal matter. Neither are they defiled with women. This does not refer to a physical state of union between male and female, however, but to the holy marriage between the soul and the indwelling Christ, an integrated state achieved beyond physical boundaries.

During this time, three angels appear, each representing a counterpart of the dragon and two subsequent beasts. In other words, the attack of the dragon and beasts signifies the purification of the body, mind, and soul, thereby transforming them from the human to the divine state. These three synonymous aspects appear as angels, although they are merely symbols. The first angel flies in the midst of John's ascended consciousness with an everlasting gospel to preach to those still bound by human passions to the flesh. The new gospel is none other than the great reality of God and mysteries of life, as revealed through the soul's entry into the resurrection. It announces that the hour of judgment has come when the soul must reap the effects of its own making (causes).

In Revelation 14:8 the second angel appears, stating that Babylon has fallen because she made all nations drink of her iniquities. This great city signifies the impurities which have governed the mind, for the mind has drunk from the intoxication of the corporeal world and filled itself with false values. The symbolism of this great city will be more fully explained in the subsequent Chapter 17 introduction.

Immediately thereafter, a third angel appears, signifying the purification of the corporeal nature, saying that anyone who follows the path of worldly ways, although bound by darkness and ignorance, must drink of the spirit (wine) of God. He advises that the wine shall not be diluted, but poured into a cup of vexation (affliction) which shall torment the soul with purification day and night. All is not lost in this terrible battle, for the spirit of God speaks to John and tells him to write; that those are blessed who surrender self-will and die in the inner Christ. These may rest from their labors and their great works will follow them.

This poignant chapter of the Apocalypse ends with the appearance of the indwelling Christ and ruler (crown) of the soul sitting on a white cloud (white-spiritual, cloud-hidden). He bears a sharp sickle, for the time has come for reaping.

The evolution of earth has now progressed sufficiently to enter into its next phase of necessity and unveiling. The three angels, representing the opposing aspects of the dragon and subsequent beasts which attacked the body, mind, and soul, now come forth from the inner temple and cry in a loud voice that the reaping should begin. The sickles are thrust deep into the soul and it is cast into a great winepress which separates the good from the evil, as the juice of a grape is separated from its skin. This purification proceeds for the space of 1,600 furlongs (miles) or until the soul has been united with the indwelling Christ and completed in overcoming the temptations of the corporeal world.

1. I looked, and lo, I saw the indwelling Christ standing on mount Sion (signifying the holy temple within the soul). With him were those who had given birth to the Lamb and passed through the halls of judgment. These were the redeemed and wore the name Yahweh (see XIV Introduction) on their fore-heads. They were the illumined and the Christed.

1. And I looked, and lo, a Lamb stood on the mount Sion, and with him an hundred forty and four thousand, having his Father's name written in their foreheads.

2. And I heard the voice of God and it was like many waters (languages) and resounded with great power (thunder). Then I heard the voice of harpers (the flow of the Spirit through the corporeal senses), and they sang a new song (New Testament pertaining to the resurrection of the Christ in all mankind).

2. And I heard a voice from heaven, as the voice of many waters, and as the voice of a great thunder: and I heard the voice of harpers harping with their harps.

3. They sang before the throne and before the indwelling Christ, and before the soul, which had entered into marriage with the Lamb through sacrifice, purification, and by transcending the four major obstacles of the mortal nature (beasts—see 4:6-9). No one could learn that song except those who had entered into the resurrection. (See 7:4 -144,000.)

3. And they sung as it were a new song before the throne, and before the four beasts, and the elders: and no man could learn that song but the hundred and forty and four thousand, which were redeemed from the earth.

4. The Christ in them had been raised through immaculate conception[1], and they were as virgins and followed the Lamb where ever he went (followed the path of righteousness thereafter). These were the redeemed among people, for their souls had restored the king dom of God and the Lamb.

4. These are they which were not defiled with woman; for they were virgins. These are they which follow the Lamb whithersoever he goeth. These were the redeemed from among men, being the first fruits unto God and unto the Lamb.

5. They spoke truth, and their souls were pure before God which abided in them.

5. And in their mouth was found no guile: for they are without fault before the throne of God.

6. Then I saw another angel fly in the midst of heaven (the consciousness of God which inter-penetrates the soul), and it revealed the hidden mysteries of the resurrection to all people, nations, tongues and kindred.

6. And I saw another angel fly in the midst of heaven, having the everlasting gospel to preach unto them that dwell on earth, and to every nation, and kindred, and tongue, and people.

7. Saying with a loud voice, "Fear God and give glory to him: for the hour of judgment has come upon the soul. Worship him who made heaven and earth, the sea, and fountains of water."

7. Saying with a loud voice, Fear God, and give glory to him; for the hour of judgment is come: and worship him that made heaven, and earth, and the sea, and the fountains of waters.

8, And there followed another angel, saying, "The false values which built the great city (Babylon—see XIV Introduction) within the subconscious mind have fallen. It was the enticement of worldly glorification which caused the soul to drink the wine of darkness and ignorance, and which led her on the path of corruptness."

9. A third angel followed them, saying with a loud voice, "Anyone who continues to follow the enticements of matter and worships those things which destroy the body, mind and soul, shall remain chained to darkness and ignorance.

10. "These shall drink from the cup of atonement which is ministered to every soul according to its deeds. And the soul shall be cleansed by the fires of purification and destruction in the presence of the indwelling Christ and his angels."

8. And there followed another angel, saying, Babylon is fallen, is fallen, that great city, because she made all nations drink of the wine of the wrath of her fornication.

9. And the third angel followed them, saying with a loud voice, If any man worship the beast and his image, and receive his mark in his forehead, or in his hand,

10. The same shall drink of the wine of the wrath of God, which is poured out without mixture into the cup of in dignation; and he shall be Tormented with fire and brimstone in the presence of the holy angels, and in the presence of the lamb.

11. The smoke (residual purification of the subconscious) of the soul's distress rose up forever. And the purifying forces rested not day or night, but continued their onslaught on those aspects of the soul which still followed after ego and self-will.

11. And the smoke of their torment ascendeth up forever and ever: and they have no rest day nor night, who worship the beast and his image, and whosoever receiveth the mark of his name.

12. "This is the patience of those who pass into the resurrection and keep the ways of heaven, and surrender self-well to divine will."

12. Here is the patience of the saints: here are they that keep the commandments of God, and the faith of Jesus.

13. I heard a voice from heaven saying to me, "Write; blessed are those who have raised he who was dead, for they are released from the chains of matter and their great works shall follow them."

13. And I heard a voice from heaven saying unto me, Write, Blessed are the dead which die in the Lord from henceforth: Yea, saith the Spirit, that they may rest from their labours; and their words do follow them.

14. And I looked, and behold I saw the over-shadow of the inner Christ, and his wisdom (golden) ruled (crown) over the soul. He carried a sharp sickle in his hand for reaping.

14. And I looked, and behold a white cloud, and upon the cloud one sat like unto the Son of man, having on his head a golden crown, and in his hand a sharp sickle.

15. And another angel [2] came out of the inner temple crying with a loud voice to him, saying "Thrust your sickle deep into the soul. Its fruits are ripe and the time has come to reap. She is to be prepared for holy marriage to the Lamb." (Final preparation of the soul to disengage from terrestrial temptation.)

15. And another angel came out of the temple crying with a loud voice to him that sat on the cloud, Thrust in thy sickle, and reap: for the time is come for thee to reap; for the harvest of the earth is ripe.

16. And the Indwelling Christ thrust his sickle deep into the soul's remaining humanness and began to reap.

16. And he that sat on the cloud thrust in his sickle on the earth; and the earth was reaped.

17. Then another angel came out of the holy temple, which is in heaven (spiritual nature of mankind), and he also had a sharp sickle (continued purification of the mind).

17. And another angel came out of the temple which is in heaven, he also having a sharp sickle.

18. And another angel came out of the altar and he had power over fire (continued purification of the sub-conscious); and he cried in a loud voice to the angel saying, "Thrust your sharp sickle in and reap the final aspects of human bondage; for her time is at hand."

18. And another angel came out from the altar, which had power over fire; and cried with a loud cry to him that had the sharp sickle, saying, Thrust in thy sharp sickle, and gather the clusters of the vine of the earth; for her grapes are fully ripe.

19. The angel thrust his sickle into the collective experiences of the soul's journey through matter (earth-vine), and cast it into the great winepress to separate the final dregs of the soul's corporeal attraction to matter (skin) from that which is divine (wine).[3]

19. And the angel thrust in his sickle into the earth, and gathered the vine of the earth, and cast it into the great winepress of the wrath of God.

20. Then the winepress, which separated the purity of the soul from its corporeal enchantments, continued to be trod. The mind (horse) became as blood under the governorship of the risen Christ (bridle) for a space of 1,600 furlongs. (The Christ and his soul counterpart—00, become one—1, and are freed from their bondage to matter—6.)

20. And the winepress was trodden without the city, and blood came out of the winepress, even unto the horse bridles, by the space of a thousand and six hundred furlongs.

The chessboard is the world;
the pieces are the phenomena of the universe;
the rules of the game are what we call the laws of nature.
The player on the other side is hidden from us.
We known that his play is always fair, just and patient.
But, we also know, to our cost,
that he never overlooks a mistake, or makes
the smallest allowance for ignorance.

—Thomas Henry Huxley

CHAPTER XV

The Seven Final Plagues

For by one Spirit are we all baptized into one body, whether
we be Jews or Gentiles, whether we be bond or free; and have
been all made to drink into one Spirit.

I Corinthians 12:13

lthough Chapter 15 is the shortest testimony in the entire Apocalypse, it is particularly electrifying because it heralds the final phase of the soul's transformation. From the moment the seven forces of cosmic law empty the seven final plagues, to the descent of the New Jerusalem, the symbolism is massive, the events almost unbelievable.

As the purgation of the soul continues, humanity can rest in the assurance that every living being will enter into the holy estate of redemption. In a world plagued by war, hatred, violence, and fear, the promise of global peace and regeneration may seem impossible, yet it has been the vision of every great prophet. Now, however, through the companion studies of science and philosophy, it is possible to prove the systematic progression of life, and with it, the fulfillment of mankind's greatest dream.

John the Beloved, who has *raised the dead,* and is possessed by the indwelling Christ, again sees seven angels symbolizing the seven forces of cosmic law, this time bearing the seven last plagues. He sees a sea of glass mingled with fire, symbolizing that vast region of the subconscious which rests between the terrestrial and celestial estate of the soul. Although this has already been penetrated by resurrected Christ, the Light (fire) of purification in the preceding chapters is now aflame. He sees those who have already completed the resurrection by overcoming the dragon (ego & self-will). They sing the song of Moses, and the song of the Christ, saying, "*Great and marvelous are your works, Lord God almighty; just and true are your ways, and all nations shall come and worship before you.*"

After this, the Ark of the Covenant, or the holy temple within the soul, is opened, and the seven angels, representing the seven purifying forces of cosmic law, come forth dressed in pure white linen and girded with golden girdles. This signifies the final struggle of the soul as it is further prepared for the dramatic conclusion of the Apocalypse. Although it has already undergone extensive purging, physically, mentally, and emotionally, and suffered grievously over its past wrong doing, it must still battle the last dregs of self-will, symbolized in the Christian mysteries *as rolling away of the stone from the front of Christ's tomb*. As the seven angels are wearing girdles wrought of gold, one can assume that these final vexations are intended to teach the soul great wisdom.

This brief chapter concludes as the firstborn (lion), or the indwelling Christ, bequeaths the seven forces with the final pestilence, after which the soul will be separated from God until absolution of its remaining unwholesomeness.

1. And I saw another sign in heaven, great and marvelous, seven angels bearing the seven powerful forces of cosmic law which would complete the final purgation of the soul.

1. And I saw another sign in heaven, great and marvelous, seven angels having the seven last plagues; for in them is filled up with the wrath of God.

2. And I saw the vast sea (sub-conscious mind) which separated the inferior and superior natures of the soul like a sea of glass (as above, so below). I saw those who had gained victory over the corporeal senses through the resurrection of the indwelling Christ, stand upon the sea (rule over the inferior nature) with harps (see 5:8), for these were now governed by divine will.

2. And I saw as it were a sea of glass mingled with fire: and them that had gotten the victory over the beast, and over his image, and over his mark, and over the number of his name, stand on the sea of glass, having the harps of God.

3. Those who had overcome the impurities of the soul sang the song of Moses (Deut.32:1-7), and of the indwelling Christ, crying, "Great and marvelous are your works, Lord God Almighty, just and true your ways. You are king, and you rule over all souls who have been redeemed (saints—those who have completed the resurrection of the dead).

3. And they sing the song of Moses the servant of God, and the song of the lamb, saying, Great and marvelous are thy works, Lord God Almighty; just and true are thy ways, thou King of saints.

4. Who shall not surrender to your perfect Law, O Lord, and glorify your name? You alone are holy, and all nations shall come to worship before you because the impurities of their souls have been made manifest.

4. Who shall not fear thee, O Lord, and glorify thy name? For thou only art holy: for all nations shall come and worship before thee; for thy judgments are made manifest.

5. After that I looked, and behold, the tabernacle of God within the soul was opened and revealed the nature of God and his divine plan.

5. And after that I looked, and, behold, the temple of the tabernacle of the testimony in heaven was opened;

6. The seven angels of cosmic forces which emanate from the throne of God came forth from the temple bearing seven plagues. They were clothed in white linen to signify further purification of the soul and girded with golden (wisdom) girdles, for the seven last plagues of atonement would endow the soul with great wisdom.

6. And the seven angels came out of the temple, having the seven plagues, clothed in pure and white linen, and having their breasts girded with golden girdles.

7. And the Lion (Indwellling Christ, or first born) would allow the seven purgations to be administered by the angels, which would accord the soul with wisdom (seven golden vials) under divine will.

7. And one of the four beasts gave unto the seven angels seven golden vials full of the wrath of God who liveth for ever and ever.

8. The soul is filled with sorrow from its indiscretion (smoke) when it beholds the glory of God, and the power of God. It cannot, however, complete the holy union until the seven last plagues have discharged their judgment.

8. And the temple was filled with smoke from the glory of God, and from his power; and no man was able to enter into the temple, till the seven plagues of the seven angels were fulfilled.

CHAPTER XVI

Vials of Wrath

There shall be a time of trouble, such as never was since there
was a nation even to that same time: and at that time
thy people shall be delivered, every one that
shall be found written in the book.

Daniel 12:1

The time has come for the soul's final purification. In the writings of St. John of the Cross, *Dark Night of the Soul*, this period is described as the second dark night, or the night of the spirit. The first period of purgation is referred to as the night of the senses, in which the soul is subdued physically, mentally, and emotionally by the spirit. The latter is a spiritual purgation, wherein the soul is cleansed and stripped according to the spirit, subdued, and made ready for union with the indwelling Christ. In the Christian mysteries it is said that Jesus fell two times on the via Dolorosa, thereby symbolizing two periods in which those who seek the resurrection of the dead must enter. These are symbolized by two gateways, the first causes the soul to move into the first dark night, and, while possessing the basic principles of all powers, it still remains somewhat enmeshed in the ego and self-will.

Ego and self-will are depicted in the earlier chapters of the Apocalypse as the war with Lucifer and the testing, or trials, which judges whether the soul is ready to enter into the holy marriage with the indwelling Christ. Later the soul reaches another gateway, or level, which moves those who have thus far successfully traversed the early trials into a world of greater wisdom, contemplation, and higher powers. This will ultimately unite the soul with its holy bridegroom. Heaven on earth (New Jerusalem) will be achieved when all people have completed the resurrection, which will herald the end of human life as it is today.

The sixteenth chapter opens with a mighty flourish, for the voice of God authorizes the seven cosmic forces to pour their vials of pestilence upon the remnant of the soul's affection for its corporeal nature. One after another, the angels obey the will of the spirit and pour their vials of calamity upon the body, mind, and soul in order to remove the last visages of the inferior nature (ego & self-will, or the dragon).

The first angel creates a grievous sore upon those aspects of human will remaining bound to the enticements of the corporeal world. The second pours his vial upon the deep regions of the subconscious and it becomes as blood[1] because of its past indiscretions. Subsequently, the third angel pours his vial upon the mind, which reflects the subconscious, and it too becomes as blood through the death of its impurities. Next, the fourth pours his upon the sun, signifying that light which is of earth, and power is given to him to purify every aspect of the soul which is subjected to the unwholesomeness of the flesh body.

There still remain additional angels which must allow their forces to descend upon the corporeal aspects of the soul's incarceration into matter. Thus, the fifth angel pours his vial upon the seat of the beast (ego & self-will), and the material kingdom is filled with darkness.

Although the soul has undergone many things by this time, the ego, or beast still has much strength. It is also difficult for the soul to understand that true mastery over the corporeal senses can only be achieved through such trials, for the less self centered it is the more divine it becomes. The more divine it is, the greater is the love, power, and wisdom of the soul, and the greater is its work. God and the indwelling Christ do not bring these woes upon mankind to make them suffer, but to heal them of those afflictions which have destroyed their peace and happiness, and to make possible a heaven on earth, mankind's ultimate achievement.

After this, the sixth angel releases his power and dries up the great revelations which have been pouring down from the throne of God (Euphrates River-see; 9:14). This is a difficult period for the soul, because direct revelation from God has nurtured it for several years. Now, even this is taken away, or appears to have been taken away, so that greater development of the individual's assignment with destiny can be furthered. Not only is it the responsibility of the soul to raise the indwelling Christ and submit to his will, but it is also the responsibility of the Christ to bring forth the brotherhood of all mankind. Thereafter, the soul, as a manifestation of consciousness of the indwelling Christ on earth, will work for the good of all life, both great and small, and fulfill its greater purpose. This, of course, explains John the Beloved's reference to preparing the way for the kings of the east, in that the east, as illustrated earlier, represents resurrection, new birth and dawn. All who enter into the resurrection are therefore looked upon as spiritual kings or rulers over their corporeal natures.

As the drama continues to unfold, John the Beloved sees three unclean spirits in the form of frogs coming out of the mouth of the dragon (ego) and the false prophet (self-will), signifying the remaining impurities of the soul, the mind, and the body, thereby correlating with the dragon and the two beasts. This symbolism is particularly amusing, because frogs were the unsavory plague of Exodus which overran Egypt, creating stench, decay and death. Although it may be difficult to equate frogs to the impurities of the soul, mind, and body, these three plagues are the real essence of mankind's malevolent character and manifest in ultimate human destruction. As these impurities come out of the mouth of the dragon (ego) and false prophet (self-will), they lead mankind into an affection for worldly ways. Therefore the soul is taken into a great battlefield where it must view the carnage of these violations and ultimately rise victorious. For this reason, the indwelling Christ solicitously cautions mankind to keep the soul's garment pure, lest it become naked and its shame be revealed.

Finally, the indwelling Christ gathers the soul into a place called Armageddon, taken from the Hebrew term *Har Megiddo,* or hill. This term was justly chosen, for Megiddo occupied a marked position on the southern rim of the plain of Esdralon and was once the greatest battlefield in Palestine. It was famous for two great victories: Barak over the Canaanites (Judges 4:14), and Gideon over the Midianites (Judges 7), as well as two great disasters; the death of Saul (I Samuel 31:8) and of Josiah (II Kings 23:29-30). In the Apocalypse 15:16, Armageddon becomes a poetical expression for the terrible and final conflict of the soul as it struggles to become divine. It is, therefore, applicable that the seventh angel now comes forth and empties his vial upon the soul, bringing great revelations and an earthquake, "such as was not since man came upon the earth."

1. I heard the voice of God speak from within the temple of the soul saying to the seven purifying forces of cosmic order, "Go your ways, and release your judgments upon the corporeal senses of mankind."

1. And I heard a great voice out of the temple saying to the seven angels, Go your ways, and pour out the vials of the wrath of God upon the earth.

2. And the first angel went forth and poured his vial upon the remaining impure aspects of the soul. A great sorrow fell upon it because of its participation in those things which bound it to darkness and caused it to follow after worldly values.

2. And the first went, and poured out his vial upon the earth; and there fell a noisome and grievous sore upon the men which had the mark of the beast, and upon them which worship his image.

3. And the second angel poured his vial upon the subconscious mind (sea and bottomless pit) causing the soul to view the balance of its past improprieties. These became as blood to the soul until all things were made pure and the last visages of mortality were exchanged for immortality (died in the sea).[2]

3. And the second angel poured out his vial upon the sea; and it became as the blood of a dead man: and every living soul died in the sea.

4. And the third angel poured his vial upon the mind and the false ideals of the soul, causing it to wander in darkness. And it was as blood flowing from a wound.

4. And the third angel poured out his vial upon the rivers and fountains of water; and they became as blood.

5. Then, I heard him say, "You are righteous Lord, who are, and was, and shall be, for your judgment is fair.

5. And I heard the angel of the waters say, Thou are righteous, O Lord, which art, and wast, and shalt be, because thou has judge thus.

6. "For they have passed through the purification of the saints and prophets, and you have administered your purgation, for they are worthy."

6. For they have shed the blood of saints and prophets, and thou hast given them blood to drink; for they are worthy.

7. And I heard another voice speak from the altar (bridge between mortal and immortal) saying, "Even so, Lord God, your judgments are true and righteous, for they have been given to every person according to their words, their deeds, and their thoughts."

7. And I heard another out of the altar say, Even so Lord God Almighty, true and righteous are thy judgments.

8. The fourth angel poured his vial upon that aspect of the soul which was still imprisoned by the material world (sun). Power was given to him to reveal the false values of the corporeal disposition (scorched with fire).

8. And the fourth angel poured out his vial upon the sun ; and power was given unto him to scorch men with fire.

9. And the soul was scorched by the purification rendered by the indwelling Christ (fire) and sought to war against the will of God, which had power over the plagues, for it surrendered not to divine intervention.[3]

9. And men were scorched with great heat, and blasphemed the name of God, which hath power over these plagues: and they repented not to give him glory.

10. When the fifth angel sounded, it poured out his vial upon the seat of the beast (ego-dragon). Those aspects of the soul still bound to self-will suffered great darkness, for it was cut away from the Light of God. Its' mortal temptations and false aspirations tormented (gnawed) it, causing great pain.

10. And the fifth angel poured out his vial upon the seat of the beast; and his kingdom was full of darkness; and they gnawed their tongues for pain.

11. Still, because of its affection to the senses, the soul blamed God for its pains and sores, and departed not from the path of self-will.

11. And blasphemed the God of heaven because of their pains and their sores, and repented not of their deeds.

12. And the sixth angel poured out his vial upon the living waters (mind), which flowed from the seat of mortality which the soul bore. The impurities of the mind were dried up, that those who had raised the dead (raised the indwelling Christ) and ruled over the ego could be prepared for the holy marriage.

12. And the sixth angel poured out his vial upon the great river Euphrates; and the water thereof was dried up that the way of the kings of the east might be prepared.

13. I saw the impurities of the body, mind, and soul come out of the mouth of the dragon (ego) and out of the mouth of the beast (mind) and out of the mouth of the false prophet (self-will).

13. And I saw three unclean spirits like frogs come out of the mouth of the dragon, and out of the mouth of the beast, and out of the mouth of the false prophet.

14. They are the last unclean aspects, which have ruled over the soul and subjected it to the rulership of worldly ways. These impurities, having their seat in the soul's humanness, now gather to do battle on the great day when the indwelling Christ had been raised from the dead.

14. For they are the spirits of devils, working miracles, which go forth unto the kings of earth and of the whole world, to gather them to the battle of the great day of God Almighty.

15. "Behold I come as a thief, and blessed are they who prepare for my coming and do not defile the soul, lest it becomes naked and must bear witness to its indiscretions."

15. Behold, I come as a thief. Blessed is he that watcheth and keepeth his garments, lest he walk naked, and they see his shame.

16. The indwelling Christ gathered the soul up into a high place of great desolation; called *Har Megiddo* (Armageddon became the poetical expression for the terrible and final conflict).

16. And he gathered them together into a place called in the Hebrew tongue Armageddon.

17. And the seventh angel poured out his vial upon the air, signifying the pouring of divine will through mortality. God spoke from within the holy temple saying, "It is done."

17. And the seventh angel poured out his vial into the air; and there came a great voice out of the temple heaven, from the throne, saying, "it is done."

18. There were great revelations within the soul and there was a great earthquake, which shook loose the final threads holding it to the temporal world of matter, the like of which had never been experienced before.

18. And there were voices, and thunders, and lightnings; and there was a great earthquake, such as was not since men were upon the earth, so mighty an earthquake, and so great.

19. The remaining impurities of the soul were divided into three parts, those of the ego (dragon), those of the mind (beast), and those of the body (2nd beast), and these were destroyed. And the soul came in remembrance before God, that she be made pure by the exactness (wine-spirit) of his perfect Law.

19. And the great city was divided into three parts, and the cities of the nations fell: and great Babylon came in remembrance before God, to give unto her the cup of the wine of the fierceness of this wrath.

20. Every obstacle fled away, and the false ideals of the soul were no more found.

20. And every island fled away, and the mountains were not found.

21. And a great hail storm (devastation) fell upon the soul from the indwelling Christ, every stone a talent (full weight which an able man can carry). That which was enchained to the material world reproached God because of this terrible plague, for the suffering was exceedingly great.

21. And there fell upon men a great hail out of heaven, every stone about the weight of a talent: and men blasphemed God because of the plague of the hail; for the plague thereof was exceedingly great.

CHAPTER XVII

Babylon—Harlot of Rome

Let every soul be subject unto the higher powers. For there is
no power but of God: the powers that be are ordained of God.
Whosoever therefore resisteth the power,
resisteth the ordinance of God:

Romans 13:1-2

abylonia is an ancient city-state on the Plain of Shinar, coming from the term Acadian Babilu (Gate of God). Its name originated from the Hebrew root Balal, meaning to confound, and refers to the confusion resulting from various languages spoken at the Tower of Babel, a meeting place for many tribes. It was founded by descendants of Cush and followers of Nimrod, but did not come into great prominence until approximately 1830 BC. The city reached its greatest period of glory under the reign of Nebuchadnezzar II (BC. 605-462), and began its decline when Nebuchadnezzar was succeeded on the throne by Amel Marduk, the Evil (BC. 562-560).

On October 13, 539 BC. Babylon fell to Cyrus of Persia, after which its deterioration eventually turned most of the region back into the desert from which it came. For this reason, John the Beloved selected Babylon to represent the carnage and corruption occurring through mankind's collective or individual violations against the ways of heaven. Just as the city had been returned to desolation because of its willful ways, so would the soul become barren because it had placed its values in the outer adornments of a temporal world.

In the imperial opening of the seventeenth chapter a remarkable woman, clothed in scarlet and purple, comes forth upon a scarlet colored beast which is full of uncleanness. The woman signifies the soul, although the outer attire represents the enticements which have held the soul captive in matter. It must be remembered that the soul is not bad, for it is an individualized aspect of God and the designated bride of the indwelling Christ. As John has often pointed out, however, its attraction to worldly things has bound it to the infirmities of old age, death, illness, ignorance, hatred, jealousy etc. Therefore, these things have kept the soul in a state of sorrow and lacking in a sense of self-worth rather than a state of peace and happiness. Unfortunately, transgressions are often deeply ingrained within the soul and these must be drawn out through a process of purgation and purification.

As the mysteries of the Apocalypse continue to unfold, both readers and scholars may perceive that the current work appears more frightening than the original and literal interpretation of this great masterpiece. It is important, however, to remember that the soul is not fighting this battle alone, but she has resurrected the indwelling Christ who is championing her through these trials of transformation.

The woman, symbolized as the city of Babylon, makes her entry on the great scarlet (sacrifice) beast with seven heads (7 epochs of corporeal progression) and ten horns (return to one) and reflects the soul's long submergence in its corporeal nature. The colors of scarlet and purple correlate with the ritualistic colors of Moses' Tabernacle in the Wilderness. The woman represents not only the soul in its corporeal imprisonment, but also an aspect which is divine (royal color purple). She is wearing gold and precious stones. In this particular instance gold does not represent wisdom, or the divine spirit, but the world of material senses which have led her down the path of sense gratification. Unfortunately, from here on the symbolism becomes even more difficult to put into words. One might say that these things are easy to perceive and most difficult to define.

The harlot has been branded, an ancient custom created to disfigure the human body for the purpose of punishment to denote slavery, or to serve as a warning. In this case, the brand is used to disfigure so that the beauty of her countenance is no longer appealing (meaning that the attractions of the corporeal world will cease). She is a symbol and therefore a mystery.

Genesis, chapters one and two, prove that the soul was sent into matter by the will of God for growth and progression. Thus the harlot signifies that which is not revealed (mystery), and because of her journey in the corporeal world she has brought the soul much defilement (abominations).

As John the Beloved marvels over the splendor of this revelation, the angel says, "Why do you marvel? I will tell you the mystery of the woman, and of the beast that carries her, which has seven heads and ten horns."

Revelation XVII:8 begins with the statement; *The beast that thou sawest was, and is not; and shall ascend out of the bottomless pit, and go into perdition.* This defines the beast as an integral part of the deeply rooted practices imbedded in the subconscious memory patterns of the soul. It must rise from its bottomless pit in order to be destroyed by the indwelling Christ. Therefore, the beast *was*, for it has been the corporeal vehicle which has enabled the human soul to experience its necessary lessons throughout progressive evolution (is not). It is not what it appears to be, for progress has brought about the compulsory cycles of necessity. Nonetheless the subconscious mind must still be purged (go into perdition) in order for the soul to ascend into the state of union with its indwelling divine counterpart.

John the Beloved further describes this ongoing and remarkable transformation of the soul by stating that he saw seven kings, of which five are fallen, one is, and the other is not yet come, referring to the fact that the creation has already passed through five epochs of planetary progression, is currently in its sixth (human), and that there is another yet to come (the seventh and final epoch which will bring forth the indwelling Christ in all mankind and heralds the descent of the new Jerusalem). One is reminded of the final verse of; *The Holy City.*

In the words of F.E. Weatherly:

> *And once again the scene was changed, New earth there seemed to be, I saw the Holy City Beside the tideless sea; The light of God was on its streets, The gates were opened wide, And all who would might enter, And no one was denied. No need of moon or stars by night, Or sun to shine by day, It was the new Jerusalem That would not pass away. (Music by Stephen Adams).*

This unusual, but touching chapter concludes with the power of the lamb presiding in victory over those who have entered into the resurrection, and over the people, multitudes, nations and tongues. In the end of the soul's struggle toward oneness, the divinity in it does come to hate its transgressions and transmutes, or destroy those things which are impure. At last it understands, with great certainty, that it was willed into matter by the power of God and that it is destined to dwell in the dense domain of human life until the corporeal lessons have been learned.

1. There came one of the seven angels, which had poured his vial upon the soul, saying, "Come hither: I will show you the judgment yet to come upon those impurities which still remain in the unconscious aspects of the soul because of its bondage to the material senses.

1. And there came one of the seven angels which had the seven vials, and talked with me, saying unto me, Come hither; I will shew unto thee the judgment of the great whore that sitteth upon many waters.

2. "These have caused those who rule over earth to commit great iniquities, for the people of the earth have become intoxicated with the enticements of worldly fame, power and wealth."

2. With whom the kings of the earth have committed fornication, and the inhabitants of the earth have been made drunk with the wine of her fornication.

3. Then he lifted my consciousness into a higher state, and into the wilderness of the subconscious which rests between mortal and immortal (the battle field of Armageddon). I saw the soul mounted upon a scarlet (sacrifice and bloodshed) beast (ego and self-will) full defilements from its journey through matter.

3. So he carried me away in the spirit into the wilderness: and I saw a woman sit upon a scarlet coloured beast, full of names of blasphemy, having seven heads and ten horns.

4. That part of the soul which was divine, was arrayed in purple (purple-ascension=merger of red-sacrifice and blue-surrender. See: Moses' Tabernacle in the Wilderness). And the soul achieved wisdom (gold cup) as it suffered, because of its wrongdoings (abominations etc.)

4. And the woman was arrayed in purple and scarlet colour, and decked with gold and precious stones and pearls, having a golden cup in her hand full of abominations and filthiness of her fornication.

5. And she was branded (material attraction marred), that the fascination which drew the senses into darkness and ignorance be diminished (see chapter introduction).

5. And upon her forehead was a name written, MYSTERY, BABYLON THE GREAT, THE MOTHER OF HARLOTS AND ABOMINATIONS OF THE EARTH.

6. I saw those aspects of the soul which had been bound to matter and intoxicated by worldly enchantment and knew not the ways of heaven and teachings of Jesus; and when I saw her I wondered with great admiration.

6. And I saw the woman drunken with the blood of the saints, and with the blood of martyrs of Jesus: and when I saw her, I wondered with great admiration.

7. And the angel said to me, "Why do you marvel? I will reveal the mystery of the woman and of the beast that carries her, which signifies the seven epochs of systematic progression(seven heads) that will ultimately raise the soul into divine union with the indwelling Christ (1-0).

7. And the angel said unto me, Wherefore didst thou marvel? I will tell thee the mystery of the woman, and of the beast that carrieth her, which hath the seven heads and ten horns.

8. "The beast which you saw is comprised of the corporeal nature of mankind, although it is not the true nature of the soul. Ego and self-will must rise from the collective experiences of the unconscious (bottomless pit) and be destroyed in order for the divinity of the soul to prevail. And those who have not raised the indwelling Christ (written in the Book of Life) will wonder greatly when they perceive that human life was a necessity (was), but is only temporal (is), and must yet prevail until all mankind has completed the resurrection of the dead (yet is).

8. The beast that thou sawest was, and is not; and shall ascend out of the bottomless pit, and go into perdition: and they that dwell on earth shall wonder, whose names were not written in the book of life from the foundation of the world, when they behold the beast that was, and is not, and yet is.

9. "The wise will know that the seven heads of the beast are the seven epochs of progressive necessity which the soul must endure.

9. And here is the mind which hath wisdom. The seven heads are seven mountains, on which the woman sitteth.

10. "Five phases of creation have been completed (fallen), but human life now prevails (is) and is the sixth (Genesis 24:31). The seventh, however, is yet to come when the indwelling Christ is raised in all mankind. And when he comes he will rule over earth for a short time, for the human cycles of necessity will be finished.

10. And there are seven kings: five are fallen, and one is, and the other is not yet come; and when he cometh, he must continue a short space.

11. "The beast symbolizes the corporeal nature of the soul which
contains the seven evolutionary
cycles of progression. Therefore it
is the eighth of the seven, and must
be overcome (self-will surrenders
to divine-will).

*11. And the beast that was, and is
not, even he is the eighth, and is of
the seven, and goeth into perdition.*

12. And the ten (fusion of the soul
with its divine counterpart-1-0)
horns which you saw symbolizes a
soul which has not yet become one
in God. Therefore, the ego and self-
will are without a kingdom until
the soul is united in marriage with
the Lamb, for these rule until the
two have be come one (one hour).

*12. And the ten horns which thou
sawest are ten kings, which have received no kingdom as yet; but receive
power as kings one hour with the
beast.*

13. "These are of the corporeal
nature, and will give power and
strength to the mind.

*13. These have one mind, and shall
give their power and strength unto
the beast.*

14. "And the indiscretions of the
soul will war against the Lamb, but
these shall be overcome, for Light
is stronger than darkness. He is
Lord of all lords and King of all
kings, and those who have entered
into the resurrection are those who
have been called and chosen, because they have been faithful to his
ways."

*14. These shall make war with the
Lamb, and the Lamb shall overcome
them: for he is Lord of lords, and
King of kings: and they that are with
him are called, and chosen, and
faithful.*

15. And he said to me, "The waters which you saw are the people, and multitudes, and nations, and tongues who are ruled over by ego and self-will and have not yet entered into the resurrection.

16. "When the indwelling Christ has been raised from the dead, he shall cause the soul to hate its impurities, and he shall cleanse her of worldly attachments (make naked). And he shall consume her remaining weaknesses and purify her with the fires of his Light.

17. "For God has ordained the soul's bondage to a corporeal nature for the sake of its maturity. It shall remain accordingly until it has been drawn into the resurrection.

18. "And that woman you saw signifies the corporeal nature (reigneth) which, having disobeyed the ways of heaven through sense enticements, has been led into war and chaos. Such governs those who now rule over the earth.

15. And he saith unto me, "The waters which thou sawest, where the whore sitteth, are people, and multitudes, and nations, and tongues.

16. And the ten horns which thou sawest upon the beast, these shall hate the whore, and shall make her desolate and naked, and shall eat her flesh, and burn her with fire.

17. For God hath put in their hearts to fulfill his will, and to agree, and give their kingdom unto the beast, until the words of God shall be fulfilled.

18. And the woman which thou sawest is that great city, which reigneth over the kings of the earth.

CHAPTER XVIII

Fall of the Harlot

*And so it is written, The first man Adam was made a living
soul; the last Adam was made a quickening spirit. How be it
that was not first which is spiritual; but that which is
natural; and afterward that which is spiritual.
The first man is of the earth, earthy: the second man is
the Lord from heaven. As is the earthy, such are they also
that are earthy: and as is the heavenly, such are they also
that are heavenly. And as we have borne the image of the
earthy, we shall also bear the image of the heavenly.*

I Corinthians 15:45-49

It would be somewhat difficult to consider this chapter
exciting, for much of the symbolism has already been
clarified. Also the long drawn out death of the harlot seems
to be repeating those things which would be well understood by
now. However, John the Beloved had a reason for his presenta-
tions, and perhaps the final death of the corporeal nature had the
same impact on him as the finale of a great symphony. For this
reason, Chapter 18 shall receive the same careful attention as all
the preceding chapters.

The primary thing to remember is that the harlot represents not only the individual consciousness, but also the collective consciousness of the world. The soul has been enmeshed by the enticements of mortality (wealth, power etc), and because of this the collective soul consciousness within cities has brought much destruction in the form of wars, violence, sickness and death due to darkness and ignorance.

John is not as fascinated by Babylon as it may appear, but she not only represented the enticements of the soul, but the future downfall of great cities and their nations. He knew that one day Jerusalem would become but a shadow of its past greatness and her people, like all people, would suffer terrible reprisals for their indiscretions. He not only tried to warn them of the forthcoming disasters by using Babylon as an example of the iniquities which resided in great cities, but also to show that these same iniquities exist in the individual soul. The outer, therefore, was a reflection of all that dwelled within. At the same time he clearly saw the child-like nature of the people and sought to instill in them the knowledge which would alleviate the suffering that lay ahead.

It becomes obvious, from John's disclosures in the Apocalypse, that most of the people would not listen, but instead continued to follow in the ways of mortal attachments and enticements. Although he tried to warn them, he also tried to leave a promise that they would ultimately overcome this nature which bound them to suffering and sorrow.

From the first verse, Chapter 18 resounds with cries of desolation, even as today's world cries over the deterioration of its great cities filled with crime, drugs, and tenements, such as London, Bombay, Los Angeles, New York, etc. Babylon is the story of any soul and any nation which has placed mortality above immortality. Perhaps the greatest consolation rests in the promise of the last three paragraphs, that the corporeal nature which has bound the soul to a material world is dying and will exist no more. Therefore, the battle is almost over and that which is lesser in mankind has been, or will be, transmuted, negated, and changed. This is an extraordinary time for the soul; although not yet quite liberated, it now perceives that the end is near.

Once freed from the fetters of the dark night, the soul, although still in human embodiment, can now fulfill its great potential. It is no longer human, but one in God through the resurrection of the indwelling Christ. The next four chapters reveal this glorious finale.

1. After these things I saw another angel descend from the high angelic regions, having great power; and that part of the soul subjected to the corporeal world was lightened with his glory.

1. And after these things I saw another angel come down from heaven, having great power; and the earth was lightened with his glory.

2. He cried mightily with a strong voice, saying, "The enchantment of the corporeal nature (Babylon) is fallen, and is the habitation of defilement, and a prison for every unclean and negative thought (an ancient symbol for thought is a bird).

2. And he cried mightily with a strong voice, saying, Babylon the great is fallen, is fallen, and is become the habitation of devils, and the hold of every foul spirit, and a cage of every unclean and hateful bird.

3. "All peoples and nations have partaken of those things which destroy the body and soul. Those who have ruled over earth have desired power over one another, have led the innocent to war, and the merchants of earth have waxed rich on unlawful gains."

3. For all nations have drunk of the wine of the wrath of her fornication, and the kings of the earth have committed fornication with her, and the merchants of the earth are waxed rich through the abundance of her delicacies.

4. And I heard the voice of the indwelling Christ, saying, "Come out of her my people and be not partakers of mortal enchantments, or you shall receive her plagues.[1]

4. And I heard another voice from heaven, saying, Come out of her, my people, that ye be not partakers of her sins, and ye receive not of her plagues.

5. "For the indiscretions of mortality have tarnished the divinity of the soul, and every violation to the ways of heaven has been seen by God. (The inner Christ dwells within mankind and has witnessed all transgressions—nothing is hidden.)

5. For her sins have reached unto heaven, and God hath remembered her iniquities.

6. "The soul must forsake the enchantment of mortality and leave it desolate, as it was made desolate and separated the soul from its true inheritance, which is the kingdom of heaven. Now it must fill the cup of transgression with double righteousness.

6. Reward her even as she rewarded you, and double unto her double according to her works: in the cup which she hath filled, fill to her double.

7. "How much the corporeal nature has glorified herself and partaken of those things which brought darkness to the soul. Now that her days are numbered, she says, 'I am queen and am no widow because mankind consorts with me, and I shall see no sorrow.' (a soul bound to matter perceives no reprisals for its transgressions in human life.)

7. How much she has glorified herself, and lived deliciously, so much torment and sorrow give her: for she saith in her heart, I sit a queen, and am no widow, and shall see no sorrow.

8. "Therefore the time now is when the worldly enchantment of the soul must reap what it has sown. Death shall come to its dishonorable ways, for the soul will cease to violate the ways of God (famine). The worldly enticements shall be burned with the fires of purification by the indwelling Christ; strong is His will that judges the impurities of the soul.

8. Therefore shall her plagues come in one day, death, and mourning, and famine; and she shall be utterly burned with fire: for strong is the Lord God who judgeth her.

9. "Those who have lived in her splendor and followed the path of corruptness shall grieve over the loss of worldly enticements and attachments, as the consciousness of the indwelling Christ (fires of purification) descends upon the self-will of the soul.

9. And the kings of the earth, who have committed fornication and lived deliciously with her, shall bewail her, and lament for her, when they shall see the smoke of her burning.

10. "And the contrary nature of mankind shall fear this dark night, saying, "Alas, alas, my forward ways of self-will have come before God, and the hour (union between the mortal and immortal) of my atonement has come.

10. Standing afar off for the fear of her torment saying, Alas, alas, that great city Babylon, that mighty city! for in one hour is thy judgment come.

11. "And that part of the soul bound to the material (merchants) world shall weep and mourn over the death of its corporeal customs, for it will not longer partake of mortality.

11. And the merchants of the earth shall weep and mourn over her; for no man buyeth their merchandise any more.

12. "The merchandise of gold, and silver, and precious stones, of pearls, and fine linen, and purple,[2] and silk, and bloodshed and thyine (citron—very expensive and well represents the material passions of the soul) wood, and all manner of rich things.

13. "And cinnamon, and odors, and ointments, and frankincense (Galganumgum resin used for incense), and wine, and oil, and fine flour, and wheat, and beasts, and sheep, and horses, and chariots, and slaves which hold the soul bondage.

14. "The passions which the soul has craved are departed from you, and all things which were dainty and goodly (temptations) are departed from you, and you shall find them no more.

15. "And the material senses (merchants) which enticed the soul into worldly riches shall be cast aside. Fearing torment, that part which binds the soul to worldly ways, sorrows over the death of its enticements.

12. The merchandise of gold, and silver, and precious stones, and of pearls, and fine linen, and purple, and silk, and scarlet, and all thyine wood, and all manner vessels of ivory, and all manner vessels of most precious wood, and of brass, and iron, and marble.

13. And cinnamon, and odours, and ointments, and frankincense, and wine, and oil, and fine flour, and wheat, and beasts, and sheep, and horses, and chariots, and slaves, and souls of men.

14. And the fruits that thy soul lusted after are departed from thee, and all things which were dainty and goodly are departed from thee, and thou shalt find them no more at all.

15. The merchants of these things, which were made rich by her, shall stand afar off for the fear of her torment, weeping and wailing.

16. "Saying, 'Alas, alas, that which clothed itself in fine linen, purple, and scarlet, and decked itself with material wealth, has passed away.'"

16. And saying, Alas, alas, that great city, that was clothed in fine linen, and purple, and scarlet, and decked with gold, and precious stones, and pearls!

17. In the union of the soul to its divine counterpart, the riches of the world have no merit. The ego (shipmaster) which presides over the corporeal senses, and thoughts (sailors), and passions of the mind which betrayed the soul (trade by sea), is now separated from that which was holy.

17. For in one hour so great riches is come to naught. And every shipmaster, and all the company in ships, and sailors, and as many as traded by sea stood afar off.

18. And there is much unhappiness within the soul as the fires of purification continue to work upon the worldly senses. And it wonders, What else is there but human existence?

18. And cried when they saw the smoke of her burning, saying, What city is like unto this great city!

19. And the lower nature of the soul mourned grievously (cast dust upon their heads), and cried, weeping and wailing, saying, "The world I once knew wherein dwelled the material pleasures (rich) of the mind (ship in the sea) has been made desolate through the resurrection of the indwelling Christ."[3]

19. And they cast dust on their heads, and cried, weeping and wailing, saying, Alas, alas, that great city, wherein were made rich all that had ships in the sea by reason of her costliness! for in one hour is she made desolate.

20. Rejoice over the fall of the self-centered nature, you who dwell in heaven and have been made holy through the resurrection of the indwelling Christ. God has avenged you on her."

20. Rejoice over her, thou heaven, and ye holy apostles and prophets; for God hath avenged you on her.

21. And a mighty angel took up a stone (stoned to death) like a great millstone (grinds grain into flour). He cast it into the subconscious sea which separates the soul from the higher consciousness of its divine counterpart, that the final in-discretions of self-will be ground to immaculacy, saying, "Therefore, with great upheaval the corporeal nature of the soul which has contained ego and self-will shall be cast away and shall no more be found."

21. And a mighty angel took up a stone like a great millstone, and cast it into the sea, saying, thus with violence shall that great city Babylon be thrown down, and shall be found no more at all.

22. The enticements of worldly things shall no longer chain the soul to the corporeal senses, nor shall the aspirations of self-will, whatever they are, be found any more. And the purification shall come to an end.

22. And the voice of harpers and musicians, and of pipers, and trumpeters, shall be heard no more at all in thee; and no craftsman, of whatsoever craft he be, shall be found any more in thee; and the sound of a millstone shall be heard no more at all in thee.

23. The light of the indwelling Christ shall be no longer bound by matter, and voice of the Christ and his bride shall no longer be imprisoned by worldliness: for it is the seduction of terrestrial life which deceived the soul.

23. And the light of a candle shall shine no more at all in thee; and the voice of the bridegroom and of the bride shall be heard no more at all in thee: for thy merchants were the great men of the earth; for by thy sorceries were all nations deceived.

24. And in her is found the sacrifice (blood) of prophets, and saints, and of those who entered into the Resurrection of the Dead (slain).

24. And in her was found the blood of prophets and of saints, and of all that were slain upon the earth.

CHAPTER XIX

Prince of Peace

Therefore judge nothing before the time, until the Lord come,
who both will bring to light the hidden things of darkness,
and will make manifest the counsels of the hearts: and
then shall every man have praise of God.

I Corinthians 4:5

The finale of the Apocalypse of John the Beloved is like a beautiful sunrise, which begins as a subtle light in the east and gradually spreads across the land. As the world is bathed in the deep orange of pungently aromatic stigmas of the purple-flowered crocus, the morning star shines brightly in the diminishing darkness. Everywhere there are sounds of life breaking free from the chains of oblivion, and a symphony rises from the throats of singing birds. As dawn gradually brings in a new day, the final chapters of Revelation bring forth the birth of God in Man. John does not rush his finale, but builds it into a mighty crescendo, equal only to those of a great composer or the final drama of a great screen play. His words concerning the descent of a new Jerusalem are not just the words of a promise, but words of reality, for mankind will one day bring forth a planet of peace from the throes of chaos.

Although the soul has not yet been united with the indwelling Christ, the hour is near as Chapter 19 opens. Eagerly the soul waits these last days in spite of the continuing inner struggle. Now, however, it looks upon the long years of transformation much like a student who is ready to graduate. A clarity encompasses it, for it understands the reasons of purgation and it stands liberated from sorrow, unhappiness, lack of self-worth, and the infirmities of human life. Above all it feels eternity's continuity and knows that human life is only temporal.

As the first rays of the morning sun touch the shores of the soul, John the Beloved states, "And after these things I heard the great sound of heavenly voices, saying, alleluia; salvation, and glory, and honor, and power unto the Lord our God. For true and righteous are his judgments."

By this time the soul has come to realize that its impurities have denied it true happiness, and that the judgment of God and the indwelling Christ has allowed no more purgation to fall upon it than absolutely necessary. It watches the smoke rise forever from the final fires of purification and prepares for its release from the duality of the two natures, as the four elements which bound it to earth fall before the throne of God through rebirth, sacrifice, resurrection, and ascension (four beasts—see 4:6-9). The soul stands arrayed in fine linen, clean and white, for it has been wretched like flax, separated, twisted, bleached, and woven, and, having passed through the resurrection of the dead, bears the righteousness of saints and has made her self ready for marriage to the indwelling Christ.

Once more, the divine nature of John opens and he beholds the white horse (mind) of illumination and enlightenment (see; 6:2); and seated upon him is the indwelling Christ in great splendor and glory. It is a breathtaking moment, for the Christ is clothed in garments of victory and bears the sword of truth and justice. His attire has changed from the early drama of the Odyssey, for he is now ruler *Jure divino* and comes forth into this final conflict already triumphant.

If this drama were taking place in a theater, the audience would see the heroine, dressed in white, standing on the edge of a great battlefield. On the ground before her lies the almost dead dragon, the beasts, and the false prophet. As they try to stand up in one last attempt to capture the fair lady, the great knight who has led the mighty armies into battle sweeps in for the final kill. Pushing his sword deeply into the ebbing life of the great villains, he kills them with one swoop of his mighty sword. Then he picks up his betrothed, the soul, and places her in front of him on the horse. As they ride away together to his golden kingdom in the sun, the vultures descend to pick at the dead carcasses.

1. And after these things I heard the voices of those who had passed through the resurrection, saying, "Alleluia; Salvation, and glory and honor, and power to the Lord our God.

1. And after these things I heard a great voice of much people in heaven, saying, Alleluia; Salvation, and glory, and honour, and power, unto the Lord our God.

2. "For true and righteous are His judgments. He has judged the impurities which enticed the soul to follow the path of false values and has defeated (avenged) the ego and self-will in those who entered into the resurrection."

2. For true and righteous are his judgments: for he hath judged the great whore, which did corrupt the earth with her fornication, and hath avenged the blood of his servants at her hand.

3. Again they said, "Alleluia." And smoke rose as the fires of purification completed its destruction of the atrocities of the soul, and the iniquities departed from her for ever and ever (rose up).

3. And again they said, Alleluia. And her smoke rose up for ever and ever.

4. And the soul rose from its imprisonment to matter (4 elements) through rebirth (lion) sacrifice (calf), surrender of self-will (face of man), and ascension (eagle), saying "Amen: Alleluias" (Hymn of Triumph).

4. And the four and twenty elders and the four beasts fell down and worshipped God that sat on the throne, saying, Amen; Alleluia.

5. A voice came out of the throne, saying, "Praise our God, all of you who serve him, and all of you who fear him, both small and great."

5. And a voice came out of the throne, saying, Praise our God, all ye his servants, and ye that fear him, both small and great.

6. I heard the voice of the great multitude which had entered into the resurrection and it was the sound of many nations (many waters) and a great thundering. They sang a Hymn of Triumph, for the Lord God Omnipotent (unlimited and universal) now reigned.

6. And I heard as it were the voice of a great multitude, and as the voice of many waters, and as the voice of mighty thunderings, saying, Alleluia: for the Lord God Omnipotent reigneth.

7. Let us be glad and rejoice, and give honor to Him: for the marriage of the indwelling Christ has come and the soul has made herself ready.

7. Let us be glad and rejoice, and give honour to him: for the marriage of the lamb is come, and his wife hath made herself ready.

8. To the soul was granted that she should be arrayed in fine linen (purified like flax fibers prepared to be made into thread), for she has been separated, bleached and woven into the righteousness of saints.

8. And to her was granted that she should be arrayed in fine linen, clean and white: for the fine linen is the righteousness of saints.

9. And he said to me, "Write, Blessed are they which are called to the marriage supper (Feast of the Passover signifying passover from human to divine) of the indwelling Christ." And he said to me, "These are the true teachings of God."

9. And he saith unto me, Write, Blessed are they which are called unto the marriage supper of the Lamb. And he saith unto me, These are the true sayings of God.

10. I fell at his feet to worship him and he said, "Do not do this, for I am your fellow servant and of your brethren who has risen from the dead through the teachings of Jesus the Christ. Worship therefore God, for the declaration of truth made by Jesus was in the spirit of prophecy concerning the perfection which is yet to come upon the earth."

10. And I fell at his feet to worship him. And he said unto me, See thou do it not: I am thy fellow servant, and of thy brethren that have the testimony of Jesus: worship God: for the testimony of Jesus is the spirit of prophecy.

11. And I entered into oneness with the consciousness of God and I beheld the illumined mind (6:2-white horse). And the risen Christ, called Faithful and True, rode forth from his entombment of matter, and in righteousness he judges and makes war.

11. And I saw heaven opened, and behold a white horse; and he that sat upon him was called Faithful and True, and in righteousness he doth judge and make war.

12. His eyes were flames of fire (purification), to search out and burn away the remaining iniquities of the corporeal senses. And he wore many crowns, for he rules over the seven epochs of human progression, and he had the name Christos[1] upon his vestry.

12. His eyes were as a flame of fire, and on his head were many crowns; and he had a name written, that no man knew, but he himself.

13. The indwelling Christ was clothed with a vesture dipped in blood because of his sacrifice, for he had descended into matter to assure the redemption of the soul. His name is Christos, revelation of all mysteries, the first born, and word of God.

13. And he was clothed with a vesture dipped in blood: and his name is called The Word of God.

14. And the souls which had passed through the resurrection of the dead followed him, for they were of the illumined mind (white horses) and had obtained absolution, and they were dressed in fine linen, white and clean.

14. And the armies which were in heaven followed him upon white horses, clothed in fine linen, white and clean.

15. And out of his mouth issued truth and justice (two edged sword), that he should attack the worldly nature of humanity and rule over all people with an iron will (see 1:13-17). He will purge the souls of all of their iniquities (winepress) with voraciousness, and he bears the atonement which the world must undergo (wrath of God).

15. And out of his mouth goeth a sharp sword, that with it he should smite the nations: and he shall rule them with a rod of iron: and he treadeth the winepress of the fierceness and wrath of Almighty God.

16. He had on his vesture and on his thigh[2] (rulership over the corporeal senses) a name written (Righteous), meaning King of Kings, and Lord of Lords.

16. And he hath on his vesture and on his thigh a name written, KING OF KINGS, AND LORD OF LORDS.

17. I saw an angel standing in the sun, signifying the day of the Light of the Law (the seventh epoch of human progression, referred to as the Sabbath): and he cried with a loud voice, saying to the messengers (fowls) that fly in heaven, "Come and gather yourselves together for the supper of the great God";[3]

17. And I saw an angel standing in the sun; and he cried with a loud voice, saying to all the fowls that fly in the midst of heaven, Come and gather yourselves together unto the supper of the great God;

18. "That you may consume the worldly ways ruling over the remaining aspects of corporeality, which binds the soul to matter. These are the impure thoughts, the impure mind which has governed the corporeal senses, and all of the remaining attachments to worldly enticement in all mankind, both free and bond, both small and great."

18. That ye may eat the flesh of kings, and the flesh of captains, and the flesh of mighty men, and the flesh of horses, and of them that sit on them, and the flesh of all men, both free and bond, both small and great.

19. And I saw the beast (self-will) which held the soul imprisoned to earth, and all of its reaming iniquities gathered together to make war against the indwelling Christ and against his army (angelic forces of purification).

19. And I saw the beast, and kings of the earth, and their armies, gathered together to make war against him that sat on the horse, and against his army.

20. The vanity of the soul was taken, and also self-will which had deceived the eyes of the soul during its sojourn in darkness and ignorance (mark of the beast—666, see; Introduction—Chapter 13), and caused it to follow the enticements of worldly ways. These were cast into the fires of purgation and destruction.

20. And the beast was taken, and with him the false prophet that wrought miracles before him, with which he deceived them that had received the mark of the beast, and them that worshipped his image. These were both cast alive into the lake of fire burning with brimstone.

21. And the last indiscretions remaining in the soul were dissolved by truth and justice, which emanated from the indwelling Christ, and who now ruled over the terrestrial nature (sitting on a horse). All of the corporeal senses were consumed.

21. And the remnant were slain with the sword of him that sat upon the horse, which sword proceeded out of his mouth: and all the fowls were filled with their flesh.

CHAPTER XX

The Second Death

God that made the world and all things therein, seeing that
he is Lord of heaven and earth, dwelleth not in temples
made with hands; For in him we live, and move,
and have our being,

Acts 17:24-28

lthough dawn is breaking over the horizon and the battle-field is strewn with the carcasses of the soul's past in-discretions, there is still one last mountain which rises between the scenes of war and the holy city wherein the great prince shall rule. This signifies the moment of final liberation, when the last remnants of the ego and self-will are bound and chained, and cast into burning fires of dissolution. One can al-most sense John's exultation as he approaches, not only his own oneness with God, but that of all mankind.

John wrote the Apocalypse on the Isle of Patmos where he obviously completed much of the personal transformation, which began during discipleship under Jesus who personified the Christ manifest in human form. During John's entrancement with the soul's victory he has not forgotten that every human being, even the most hardened criminal, shall one day be purified and will enter into the New Jerusalem. Thus, he continues to build this into one last, great, climactic chorus of hope and salvation for all the world.

As the pages of Chapter 20 bear witness to the final death of the soul's last visage of ego, the symbolism becomes very complex. However, much that is revealed is already well known. Therefore, readers should not allow the finale to become overwhelming. Rather they should hold these glorious moments close to their hearts. When life becomes difficult, each human being should remember not only that a new world awaits them in the dawn of tomorrow, but they are its builders.

In Revelation 20:1, John sees an angel come down from heaven, having the key to the bottomless pit (subconscious mind) and a great chain in his hand. He lays hold of the last remnants of the ego and self-will (personified by the Devil, or Satan) and binds them until the body, soul, and spirit become one (1-000 years). The great chain is forged from the revelations and truths that have descended upon the soul during its dark night. Although the inherent tendencies which have brought forth such suffering have been defeated, the body, emotions, feelings, and intellect must now bear the Christed soul (unity between the indwelling Christ and soul) and manifest its great work on earth while still in embodiment. For, this reason the wily old devil is merely chained and thrown into the fire and brimstone. He must do only good for the remainder of the soul's sojourn in flesh (tormented).

As John the Beloved continues with the Apocalypse, he sees an angel place a seal upon the dragon, that he should deceive the nations no more until a thousand years have passed. The seal is that of a cross, or mortal bondage through the cohesive force of the four elements. In the past, ego and self-will have ruled over the soul and caused it to follow the path of worldly desires. Now the tables are turned, for the dragon must henceforth submit to the greater will. Although the indwelling Christ was imprisoned in matter during the soul's attraction to matter, (referred to as the first death), he was then raised in the soul during the first resurrection. At that time all the latent impurities (accrued because of the soul's affinity for the material world) come onto the battlefield to make war (dragon loosed for the season) against the indwelling Christ, but he is victorious and the soul forsakes its mortality, referred to not only as the second death, but also the second resurrection, or liberation.

There is one other rather complex symbol in chapter 20 which is found in verse 8. The first reference is to Satan being loosed, as described in the foregoing paragraph. Next he goes forth to deceive nations which are in the four quarters of the earth. Although these cities merely reflect the self-centered nature of the ego which has been created through the soul's temporal habitation in the terrestrial world (4 elements), there is an added ingredient involved, Gog and Magog. Here John refers to Ezekiel's prophecy in the Old Testament (Ez.38:11, 14, 16, 18; 39:1). According to history, Ezekiel said Gog would invade the restored land of Israel from a far distant northern land in the last times with a powerful army of many nations. Gog would be destroyed by a wrathful judgment from the Lord, so that the nations would know that God is Lord.

Although the names Gog and Magog are allegorical (Gog referring to the prince of Rosh, Mesheck, and Tubal, and Magog referring to the land of Lydia), the battle itself refers to Ezekiel's vision of the divine destruction precipitated at the climax of the final attempt to destroy the remnant of Israel in Jerusalem and Palestine. The entire prophecy belongs to the *Day of the Lord* and includes the last revolt of nations at the close of the mediatorial messianic kingdom. This apocalyptic prophesy, greatly misunderstood in fundamental interpretation, also refers to the coming of a messianic kingdom and precedes the Apocalypse of John by many years. John uses Gog in Revelation 20:8 to represent the fulfillment of Ezekiel's prophecy depicting the victory of good over evil, light over darkness, and the divine will over self-will.

The beauty of this chapter is best summed up by its final verse, *"And whosoever was not found written in the book of life was cast into the lake of fire."*

Perhaps the following words are better suited to the modern mind: "and those who had not crossed the boundary between the mortal and immortal were cast into the Christ light of purification, that they might also enter into the resurrection of the dead."

> *But fear not thou: Men of heav'n only rare,*
> *Taught by divine nature what to embrace:*
> *Which if purif'd thou all I name shall gain*
> *And keep thy soul clear from the body's stain.*
>
> *In time of Pray'r and cleansing, eats deny'd*
> *Abstain from; thy mind rains let reason guide.*
> *Then stripped of flesh up to free ether soar,*
> *a deathless God, Divine, mortal no more*

Pythagorus-Lactantius
translated by Thomas Stanley (1625-1678)

1. I saw an angel come down from heaven having power (key) over the deep regions of the subconscious mind and he carried a great chain wrought from the soul's journey through matter.

1. And I saw an angel come down from heaven, having the key of the bottomless pit and a great chain in his hand.

2. He laid hold of the ego and self-will (dragon/Satan) which had caused darkness and death, and made it an instrument of divine will as the body, soul, and spirit became one.

2. And he laid hold on the dragon, that old serpent, which is the Devil and Satan, and bound him a thousand years.

3. And he incarcerated that part of the soul which had been enticed by the enchantment of the corporeal world, and marked it with a cross (bondage by the four elements which created matter) so that the temptations of the flesh could no longer deceive the soul until its oneness with the indwelling Christ was fulfilled: After this, the lower nature (Satan) must be loosed for the period of atonement in order to be changed.[1]

3. And cast him into the bottomless pit, and shut him up, and set a seal upon him, that he should deceive the nations no more, till the thousand years should be fulfilled: and after that he must be loosed a little season.

4. Judgment descended upon those things which still ruled over the soul's fascination for worldly things; and those who entered into the resurrection of the dead no longer walked in darkness because they had overcome the temptations of the flesh. They lived and reigned with the indwelling Christ forever (union of the body, soul, and spirit—1-000 years).

5. But those who had not yet raised the dead did not live again until unification with the indwelling Christ was accomplished. This is the first resurrection (see; Introduction XX).

6. Blessed and holy is he that enters into the resurrection, for the death of the ego and self-will (second death)[2] has no power. These shall become emissaries of God and the indwelling Christ, and shall reign with him forever (1-000).

7. And after they have raised the indwelling Christ, through the union of the body, soul and spirit, the iniquities of the soul will be let out of its prison for a short time (see; 20:3-1).

4. And I saw thrones, and they sat upon them, and judgment was given unto them: and I saw the souls of them that were beheaded for the witness of Jesus, and for the word of God, and which had not worshipped the beast, neither his image, neither had received his mark upon their foreheads, or in their hands; and they lived and reigned with Christ a thousand years.

5. But the rest of the dead lived not again until the thousand years were finished. This is the first resurrection.

6. Blessed and holy is he that hath part in the first resurrection: on such the second death hath no power, but they shall be priests of God and of Christ, and shall reign with him a thousand years.

7. And when the thousand years are expired, Satan shall be loosed out of his prison,

8. And they shall go out to deceive those which still remained imprisoned by the four elements to matter, Gog (lower nature and anti-christ) and Magog (hell, or material bondage. See; Introduction XX), to gather them together for the great battle: the number of whom is as the sand of the sea.

8. And shall go out to deceive the nations which are in the four quarters of the earth, Gog and Magog, to gather them together to battle: the number of who is as the sand of the sea.

9. The iniquities of mankind rose from the deep regions of the material senses and sought to lay waste to the divine estate (holy city) [3] wherein dwells the saints. And the fire of purification descended from the indwelling Christ, and destroyed them.

9. And they went up on the breadth of the earth, and compassed the camp of the saints about, and the beloved city: and fire came down from God out of heaven, and devoured them.

10. The terrestrial principle, which deceived the soul, was cast into the great fires of purification and desolation (brimstone), with the ego and self-will, and it was henceforth subjected to divine will day and night for ever and ever.

10. And the devil that deceived them was cast into the lake of fire and brimstone, where the beast and the false prophet are, and shall be tormented day and night for ever and ever.

11. And I saw a great white throne (the Light from which emanates the consciousness of God), and Him that sat on it, in whose countenance both heaven and earth were dissolved: and there was found no place for the remaining impurities of the soul at all.

11. And I saw a great white throne, and him that sat on it, from whose face the earth and heaven fled away; and there was found no place for them.

12. I saw those who had not yet wakened, small and great, called forth to the resurrection and they stood before God. And their souls which bore the works (collective consciousness-books) because of their sojourn in matter were opened and they were each (book) judged according to their works. (Book of Life—see—Apocalypse 5)

12. And I saw the dead, small and great, stand before God; and the books were opened: and another book was opened, which is the book of life: and the dead were judged out of those things which were written in the books, according to their works.

13. And the great waters wherein dwelled the regions of non-remembrance revealed their past indiscretions; and those who dwelled in death and hell (those whose crimes and habits have chained the soul to such darkness that they dwell in carnality and violence) were delivered up: and they were judged every man according to their works.

13. And the sea gave up the dead which were in it; and death and hell delivered up the dead which were in them: and they were judged every man according to their works.

14. And the violations which committed the soul to darkness and ignorance were cast into the great fire of purification. This is the second death (see—20:6).

14. And death and hell were cast into the lake of fire. This is the second death.

15. And whosoever had not yet entered into the resurrection of the dead was drawn forth to be purified.

15. And whosoever was not found written in the book of life was cast into the lake of fire.

CHAPTER XXI

The Final Curtain

*And God shall wipe away all tears from their eyes; and
there shall be no more death, neither sorrow, nor crying,
neither shall there be any more pain: for the
former things are passed away.*

Revelation 21:4

The great masterpiece of John the Beloved opens its
final pages with the soul's ultimate victory over matter
and the prophesy of a new world yet to come. Although
there remains one more chapter in the Odyssey, this one truly
encompasses the nucleus and the glory of Revelation. John does
not disappoint the world with a flat, simplified finale, but writes
in a manner which would appeal to the world's greatest compos-
ers and playwrights. He creates ecstasy and impatience: ecstasy,
because everyone who opens the pages of his genius will know
that they shall also one day enter a New Jerusalem; impatience,
because the fulfillment of the covenant lies ahead in the ever evolv-
ing maturity of the human race.

The symbolism in Chapter 21 is massive, perhaps even more
so than that of the preceding chapters. It is also more complex
and the hours of research to pierce the inner sanctuary of the

most guarded mysteries of Christendom can no longer be numbered. Yet, this is the sun which carries the soul through the trials of life, and later, the trials of the resurrection. The union of the soul with God is not just John's Revelation, but it breathes through the wonder of creation, Moses' covenant at Sinai, and the life of Jesus the Christ. It is the reason for and the purpose of human existence. Therefore, when the souls of all people have won the mighty battle of Armageddon and defeated the ways of ego and self-will, indeed a new world, based on brotherly love, shall be born from the ashes of mortality.

The final pages of this historic manuscript open with the descent of the New Jerusalem. John's description of the holy city is based upon the ancient Mosaic mysteries relating to Moses' Tabernacle in the Wilderness. Important keys for interpreting both structures can be found in original Hebrew, as well as the hidden teachings of Christianity.

The tabernacle of God was designed to represent the soul's indwelling perfection (the indwelling Christ) which exists in the wilderness of humanity's corporeal nature. Now that the indwelling Christ has been raised and has wrought a glorious victory on the battlefield of transformation, he will unite with the soul in holy union.

St. John of the Cross describes this spiritual marriage thusly;

> *The soul has entered this state because it has detached itself from all temporal and natural things. When the soul has lived for some time as the bride of the Son, in perfect and sweet love, God calls it and leads it into his flourishing garden for the celebration of the spiritual marriage. The two natures are so united; that which is divine is so communicated to that which is human, that without undergoing any essential change, each seems to be God.*

As a new heaven and new earth are born through oneness with the indwelling Christ, the first heaven and earth pass away, for these have been subject to human idealism which have bound the soul to death, old age, pain, and the hardships of human life. From this moment on, the soul will dwell in a heavenly estate although still in human embodiment, and be one with God forever. Revelation 21:7 reveals the mystique of this transformation when God says, "He that overcometh shall inherit all things; and I will be his God, and he shall be my son."

Shortly thereafter, the seventh angel which released the seven final purgations (see 15:1) takes John, in spirit, into a state of ascended consciousness to show him the holy city and the bride of the Lamb. This again is not a physical city, but a divine legacy and a light within the soul which contains the countenance of God.

The term jasper stone is first mentioned here, because it is an opaque and impenetrable gem signifying Savior at the head of all heavenly flocks. This gives some indication of what is to come, for the indwelling Christ must be released from his imprisonment in matter before the soul can be reborn. Therefore, the high wall containing twelve gates, guarded by the heads of the twelve tribes of Israel, represents twelve precise steps of transformational change the soul undergoes to unite with its divine counterpart (two become one-12).

The great wall surrounding the New Jerusalem signifies the risen Christ who will protect the soul from all adversity. It contains twelve gates, three on the east, signifying resurrection, three gates on the north, signifying sacrifice (death) of the personal life, three gates on the south, signifying surrender to divine will; and three gates on the west, signifying the ascension, or the exchange of mortality for immortality;. These correlate with the four beasts around the throne of God, the four horses of the Apocalypse (6:1-8), and the holy city pertaining to the throne of God (see 4:5-8).

The above directions also substantiate the divine metamorphosis of the soul, for east represents new birth, or spring; south, maturity and summer; west, old age and fall; north, death and winter;. As previously mentioned, the guardians of the four walls of the holy city, symbolized by the heads of the twelve tribes of Israel, signify twelve purgations the soul experiences during the dark night as it strives to unite with the indwelling Christ. These will be further explained in dealing with the twelve foundations of the wall of the New Jerusalem, for the semi-precious gems in the foundations bear similar interpretation to those represented by the twelve stones of the Hebrew breastplate (Exodus, Chapter 28).

John states that the Holy City is foursquare and the length is as large as the breadth and height, and measures twelve thousand furlongs (see; 14:20, 1,600 furlongs), or one hundred forty-four thousand. By this time these symbols should be very familiar, with the exception of the term foursquare. This is a particularly delightful exemplification, for the cross (four elements) which bound the soul and the indwelling Christ to matter has been transcended. Therefore the four elements (four beasts) surrender before the throne of God as the indwelling Christ and his counterpart are united, and therefore move outward from the central point to form a perfect square (see; 4:10), also referred to as the four square church,

The forgoing can be summed up quite simply by stating that the soul, now one with the Christ, has been liberated from its prison of matter, and the two shall dwell in heavenly estate within God forever and ever.

The hours of research involved in the specific placement of the precious stones used in the foundation of the great wall, as well as that of their symbolism, can no longer be numbered. Although these correlate with those found in the breastplate of the Hebrew priest during the time of Moses, some vary in physical description and order of setting. There are also some variances between Old Testament Exodus 28:17-20, Exodus 39:10-13, and Josephus Flavius' *Antiquities of the Jews* 3:vii-2. Because of John's thoroughness and exactness in all things, however, it seems appropriate to present the jewels in the exact order they appear in his Apocalypse. In any event, the layers of the foundation, like the stones of the Hebrew breastplate, represent certain phases of the resurrection.

The first layer of the foundation is a jasper stone. This designates supreme will, for the resurrected Christ must rule over the corporeal nature if there is to be a new world. As previously mentioned, the jasper is an opaque and impenetrable gem, which in ancient times signified the Savior who was placed at the head of all heavenly flocks. It is interesting to note that this stone was placed last on the Hebrew breastplate and represented victory.

The second layer of the foundation is sapphire, a blue stone used to represent the tribe of Nephthalim, and imports God-man incarnate in beast, as well as the sacred vehicle of divinity. Thus the soul, having surrendered its personal life, now receives the descent of the spirit into the flesh.

The third layer of the foundation is chalcedony, a grayish quartz stone often flecked with particles of sapphire. This conveys two small children, or two natures from one womb.

The fourth layer of the foundation is emerald, a brilliant transparent green beryl, signifying the raising of the indwelling Christ through divine birth.

The fifth layer of the foundation is sardonyx, or onyx, normally containing layers of red carnelian. In ancient times it was used to depict the signature of the Christ and his return to power and glory.

The sixth layer of the foundation is sardius, a variety of chalcedony which is a clear, translucent, and deep orange-red. In the Hebrew breastplate it was used to signify the tribe of Reuben, and represented the balance of human and divine will. Thus the soul, having given divine birth and restored the Christ to his heavenly abode, must now face the struggle of the personal versus the impersonal life.

The seventh layer of the foundation is the chrysolyte, a beryl (mineral) called gold stone, but known in modern times as a yellow topaz. It signifies the soul's entry into the halls of judgment where the law of cause and effect will purge it according to its works, similar to the manner with which gold is extracted from the earth.

The eighth layer of the foundation is beryl, a mineral essentially of aluminum beryllium silicate occurring in hexagonal (6) prisms, and signifies the sixth epoch of progressive necessity. This portends the raising of the serpent (ego & self-will), as the soul continues its struggle between human-will and divine will, and overcomes its venomous nature in order to fly like an eagle toward its heavenly estate.

The ninth layer of the foundation is topaz, an aluminum silicate mineral called peridot, denoting the rise of the soul from the body of the beast into mystical union with the indwelling Christ.

The tenth layer of the foundation is a chrysoprasus, or apple-green chalcedony with gold spots. This stone represents the resurrection of Christ from the marshlands of human will.

The eleventh layer in the foundation is a jacinth, a silicate of zirconia, signifying eternal life and living waters.

The last layer of the wall's foundation surrounding the New Jerusalem is amethyst, a transparent purple quartz, symbolizing the purple robes of ascension. Now the indwelling Christ and his divine counterpart, the soul, merge as one in God and dwell in the heavenly abode (New Jerusalem) forever.

Symbolically, the intricacies of the great wall actually sum up the soul's liberation and divine union, as outlined in the twenty preceding chapters. The mystery is not yet over, however, for John the Beloved now speaks of twelve gates as twelve pearls, every three gates as one pearl, and the streets of the city as pure gold.

The soul's passage through the *resurrection of the dead*, as outlined in the layers of the outer walls of the holy city, has endowed it with great wisdom (pearls). These twelve pearls can be broken down by dividing the number twelve by four, signifying the four great states of wisdom which foreshadow the soul's liberation through rebirth, sacrifice, resurrection, and ascension (see; four horses of the Apocalypse 6:1-8)

> *And the city had no need of the sun, neither the moon, to shine in it: for the glory of God did lighten it, and the Lamb is the light thereof.*

Revelation 21:23

1. I saw a new heaven and new earth, for the first heaven and earth, based on temporal concepts of the corporeal mind, had passed away. And the soul and the indwelling Christ became one in God and there was no more sea (subconscious mind with its accumulative violations to the way of heaven) dividing the two worlds.

1. And I saw a new heaven and a new earth: for the first heaven and the first earth were passed away; and there was no more sea.

2. And I, John, saw the holy city, the New Jerusalem, born through the resurrection of the Christ within all mankind, descend into the corporeal world. And the purified souls were as a bride adorned for her husband.

2. And I John saw the holy city, new Jerusalem, coming down from God out of heaven, prepared as a bride adorned for her husband.

3. Then I heard a great voice within me say, "Behold, the tabernacle of God is now within all mankind and he will henceforth dwell with them, and they shall be his people, and he shall be with them forever and be their God.

3. And I heard a great voice out of heaven saying, Behold, the tabernacle of God is with men, and he will dwell with them, and they shall be his people, and God himself shall be with them, and be their God.

4."And God shall wipe away all the tears from there eyes. There shall be no more death, neither sorrow, nor crying, and there shall be no more pain: for all these things will have passed away."

4. And God shall wipe away all tears from their eyes; and there shall be no more death, neither sorrow, nor crying, neither shall there be any more pain: for the former things are passed away.

5. And God, who now dwelled resplendent in the soul said, "Behold I make all things new." And he said to me, "Write: for these words are true and eternal.

5. And he that sat upon the throne said, Behold I make all things new. And he said unto me, Write; for these words are true and faithful.

6. He said to me, "The soul has now completed its great work, and I, who have been since the beginning am also the end. I will give freely to those who seek the mysteries of this transformation from human to divine.

6. And he said unto me, It is done. I am Alpha and Omega, the beginning and the end. I will give unto him that is athirst of the fountain of the water of life freely.

7. "He who overcomes the enticements of the corporeal world shall inherit all things, for he shall become as my son in which all miracles can manifest and all powers be born, and I shall be his God (see Genesis 2:1-4).

7. He that overcometh shall inherit all things; and I will be his God, and he shall be my son.

8. "But those who have not yet entered into the resurrection, because they are unbelieving and still seek after those things of the corruptible world, shall also be cast into the Light of the indwelling Christ for purgation and the second death" (see 20:6)

8. But the fearful, the unbelieving, and the abominable, and murderers, and whoremongers, and sorcerers, and idolaters, and all liars, shall have their part in the lake which burneth with fire and brimstone: which is the second death.

9. And there came to me the seventh angel which had borne the seven vials full of the last seven plagues (see 15:6-7) and talked with me saying, "Come with me and I will show you the soul which has become the bride of the Lamb."

9. And there came unto me one of the seven angels which had the seven vials full of the seven last plagues, and talked with me, saying, Come hither, I will shew thee the bride, the Lamb's wife.

10. Then, I was received into oneness with God and shown the great empire which was destined for humanity, the descent of the holy Jerusalem because of the birth of Christ in all mankind. And I saw that it was of God.

10. And he carried me away in the spirit to a great and high mountain, and shewed me that great city, the holy Jerusalem, descending out of heaven from God.

11. The soul, having the glory of God, was pure white light and like unto that of a jasper, precious and impenetrable. Victorious over matter it reflected the will God.

11. Having the glory of God: and her light was like unto a stone most precious, even like a jasper stone, clear as crystal;

12. And the indwelling Christ was the wall around the city, great and high. There were twelve gates, signifying the union of the soul and her divine counterpart (1-2), the soul having passed through the twelve necessary phases of purgation. These bore the names of the twelve tribes of Israel.[1]

12. And had a wall great and high, and had twelve gates, and at the gates twelve angels, and names written thereon, which are the names of the twelve tribes of the children of Israel:

13. There were three gates on the east wall proclaiming the resurrection of the indwelling Christ; three gates on the north signifying death to worldly imprisonment through sacrifice and atonement; three gates on the south proclaiming surrender to divine will; and three gates on the west to signify ascension, or oneness with God through the raising of the indwelling Christ; (four progressive stages which prepare the soul to unite with its divine counterpart).

13. And on the east three gates; on the north three gates; on the south three gates; and on the west three gates.

14. And the great wall which surrounded the soul contained twelve foundations, and in them the names of the twelve apostles.[2]

14. And the wall of the city had twelve foundations, and in them the names of the twelve apostles of the Lamb.

15. And he that talked with me had a gold (symbol for spiritual wisdom) reed (six cubits-bound to the sixth epoch of soul progression) to measure the soul/souls, and the gates, and the walls. (The soul/souls are evaluated to insure its readiness to rule over the terrestrial world).

15. And he that talked with me had a golden reed to measure the city, and the gates thereof, and the wall thereof.

16. The kingdom of the indwelling Christ and the soul was found to be free from human bondage, and judged perfect because the two had become one through the divine union of its subjective parts (perfection 12 x12 x12). (see 21—Introduction).

16. And the city lieth foursquare, and the length is as large as the breadth: and he measured the city with the reed, twelve thousand furlongs. The length and breadth and the height of it are equal.

17. And the measurement determined that the soul/souls was now perfected, for it measured 144,00 (see 7:4) cubits, and the soul, which had once been bound to the sixth epoch of progression, or human, (measurement of man) was now an angel.

17. And he measured the wall thereof, an hundred and forty and four cubits, according to the measure of a man, that is, of the angel.

18. And the establishment of the indwelling Christ was impenetrable as a jasper stone; His temple was pure as gold and a reflection of God's will (clear glass).

18. And the building of the wall of it was of jasper: and the city was pure gold, like unto clear glass.

19. The foundations of the indwelling Christ which the soul had raised from the dead were garnished with all manner of precious stones (see 21-Introduction): jasper, Savior who rules over all heavenly flocks; sapphire, Godman incarnate in corporeality; chalcedony, resurrection of the dead; emerald, divine birth.

19. And the foundations of the wall of the city were garnished with all manner of precious stones. The first foundation was jasper; the second, sapphire; the third, a chalcedony; the fourth an emerald.

20. The fifth, Ssrdonyx, Christ has returned to power and glory; the sixth, sardius, self-will has surrendered to divine will; the seventh chrysolyte, judgment has been rendered; the eighth, beryl, the venomous aspects of worldly ways have been transcended; the ninth topaz, the soul is raised from the marshlands of human will; the tenth, the chrysoprasus, the scales of balance between human and divine will; the eleventh, jacinth, the soul is now eternal and possesses the living waters; the twelfth, amethyst, victory and ascension.

20. The fifth, sardonyx; the sixth, sardius; the seventh, chrysolite; the eighth, beryl; the ninth, a topaz; the tenth, a chrysoprasus; the eleventh, a jacinth; the twelfth, an amethyst.

21. And the twelve gates were twelve maturations of the soul's transformation (see 21:12); and every three gates were one pearl, signifying rebirth, sacrifice, resurrection and ascension (see 4:7, four beasts around the throne of God): and the street was gold (spiritual nature raised from worldly bondage), and reflected the perfect will of God (glass).

21. And the twelve gates were twelve pearls; every several gate was of one pearl: and the street of the city was pure gold, as it were transparent glass.

22. And I saw no temple therein, for the Lord God and the indwelling Christ were now the temple of the soul.

22. And I saw no temple therein: for the Lord God Almighty and the Lamb are the temple of it.

23. And the holy city which had been built without hands was no longer bound by the ways of the flesh (sun), or the impurities of the mind (moon), for the glory of God lighted the soul, and the indwelling Christ is the light thereof.

23. And the city had no need of the sun, neither of the moon, to shine in it: for the glory of God did lighten it, and the Lamb is the light thereof.

24. And all nations shall become one in God: and those who once ruled earth shall bring their glory and honor into it.

24. And the nations of them which are saved shall walk in the light of it: and the kings of the earth do bring their glory and honour into it.

25. And there shall be no separation between heaven and earth, for there shall be no night there (no further descent into matter which brings darkness and unknowing).

25. And the gates of it shall not be shut at all by day: for there shall be no night there.

26. And the resurrected of all nations shall bring glory and honor to earth.

26. And they shall bring the glory and honor of the nations into it.

27. And nothing can enter into this divine estate which can defile, make unclean, or which is untrue. Only those may enter who have passed through the resurrection of the dead and raised the indwelling Christ. These are no longer bound by the material world, for they have gained victory over earth and are one with the Lamb and one in God.

27. And there shall in no wise enter into it any thing that defileth, neither whatsoever worketh abomination, or maketh a lie: but they which are written in the Lamb's book of life.

CHAPTER XXII

Light of the Apocalypse

But as it is written, Eye hath not seen, nor ear heard, neither
have entered into the heart of man, the things which
God hath prepared for them that love him.

Corinthians 2:9

As the great drama of St. John's Revelation drops its final curtain, a subtle quiet permeates the audience. It is as though a mighty chord has been struck, and now its faint echo imperceptibly fades into some invisible and intangible ether of another world. As the last scenes are enacted there is a moment of glory, a moment of fear, a moment of disbelief, and a moment of hope. Is it indeed possible that the curtain will rise again, not in the pages of a book, not on the transformation of John the Beloved, but within the soul of every human?

According to the Apocalyptic revelation, the hands of war will soon be stilled, and a peace treaty will be signed between humanity and God. Then shall all people walk as brothers and sisters over earth and bid farewell to the pains of mortal suffering. This shall be, as this is the cause of birth and death, pleasure and pain.

Thus, it is almost with sadness that this author closes the tempestuous pages of the Apocalypse, for the electrifying splendor of each word will leave a mark upon every soul which can never be removed. Perhaps their echo shall now join those of John the Beloved, and perhaps the notes of the symphony shall be played again and again in the morning sun, in the sound of the birds, and in the beauties of earth, but greatest in the forthcoming resurrection of all mankind.

The state is now set for the sweetness of farewell. The curtain opens upon a pure river, the water of life, which proceeds out of the throne of God. The soul stands resplendent in a garment, no longer of white linen but of brilliant white light, because He who bears it is now one with the soul which raised him from the dead. His light is the cloak, and there no longer remains any separation between the soul and the indwelling Christ. On either side of this puissant river of life stands a tree of life which bears the twelve purgations of the soul (see 21:19-20), and yields its fruit as the soul passes through transformation to become one in God through the glory of the inner Christ (1-2 months). The leaves, symbolizing the healing properties of medicinal herbs and essence of God (tree), are for the healing of nations, and there shall be no more human suffering.

As John imports this aspect of his vision, he speaks regarding the curse of Adam (prototype of the human race submerged in matter) who partook of the forbidden fruit of knowledge (good and evil), and entered into the darkness and ignorance of eve (dusk or sunset), or night, which bound the soul to mortality. Now this blindness is lifted and gone is the pain of human expression, for the soul is no longer bound to darkness and unknowing.

1. And he showed me the pure stream of life which ran from the inner sanctuary of God and indwelling Christ into the corporeal world, and it was clear as crystal because earth had become a reflection of heaven.

1. And he shewed me a pure river of water of life, clear as crystal, proceeding out of the throne of God and of the Lamb.

2. In the midst of the street which linked heaven and earth, on both sides of the river of life, stood a tree of life bearing twelve purifications which the soul had undergone as it passed through the resurrection of the dead (see 21:19-20).

2. In the midst of the street of it, and on either side of the river, was there the tree of life, which bare twelve manner of fruits, and yielded her fruit every month: and the leaves of the tree were for the healing of nations.

3. And the curse on Adam (prototype of collective man-original Hebrew) which bound him to the darkness of eve (darkness of night and bondage to matter), was no more, for God and indwelling Christ now dwell therein and all who have passed through the resurrection serve him.

3. And there shall be no more curse: but the throne of God and of the Lamb shall be in it; and his servants shall serve him:

4. They shall see his face; and they shall bear his name upon their foreheads (see; 3:12)

4. And they shall see his face; and his name shall be in their foreheads.

5. There shall be no more darkness and ignorance; and the nights (candle) and days (sun) of mortality will pass away; for the Lord God gives them light and they shall rule for ever and ever.

6. Then, he said to me, "These teachings are faithful and true: And God, who taught the holy prophets, has sent me to show those who follow Him the things which must shortly be done.

7. "Behold, I come quickly: blessed is he who lives according to those things which have been revealed in this book."

8. I, John, saw these things, and heard them. And when I had heard and seen, I fell down to worship before the feet of him who had revealed them to me.

9. He said to me, "Do not kneel before me; for I am your fellow servant, and a brother to the prophets, and of those who walk the path of righteousness and abide by the will of God."

5. And there shall be no night there; and they need no candle, neither light of the sun; for the Lord God giveth them light: and they shall reign for ever and ever

6. And he said unto me, These sayings are faithful and true: and the Lord God of the holy prophets sent his angel to shew unto his servants the things which must shortly be done.

7. Behold, I come quickly: blessed is he that keepeth the sayings of the prophecy of this book.

8. And I John saw these things, and heard them. And when I had heard and seen , I fell down to worship before the feet of the angel which shewed me these things.

9. Then saith he unto me, See thou do it not: for I am thy fellow servant, and of thy brethren the prophets, and of them which keep the sayings of this book: worship God.

10. And he said to me, "Do not hide the secrets of this prophecy, for now is the time to reveal it to the world.

10. And he saith unto me, Seal not the sayings of this prophecy of this book: for the time is at hand.

11. "He who is unjust, let him be unjust still: and he which is filthy, let him be filthy still: and he that is righteous, let him be righteous still: and he that is holy, let him be holy still.

11. He that is unjust, let him be unjust still: and he which is filthy, let him be filthy still: and he that is righteous, let him be righteous still: and he that is holy, let him be holy still.

12. "For behold, I come quickly; and my reward is with me, for every person shall reap according to their work.

12. And, behold, I come quickly, and my reward is with me, to give every man according as his work shall be.

13. "I am the indwelling Christ, who descended into matter in the beginning, and who has now been raised from the dead and shall rule forever. I am the beginning and the end.

13. I am Alpha and Omega, the beginning and the end, the first and the last.

14. "Blessed are those who abide by the will of God, for they shall enter into the resurrection of the dead and through the gates (unity of the soul and indwelling Christ) of immortality.

14. Blessed are they that do his commandments, that they may have right to the tree of life, and may enter in through the gates into the city.

15. "Without are those who do not abide by the ways of heaven and follow the path of self-will. And those who follow after them are bound by mortal deception.

15. For without are dogs, and sorcerers, and whoremongers, and murderers, and idolaters, and whosoever loveth and maketh a lie.

16. "I, the root and offspring of David, have sent my angel to reveal these mysteries which must be taught in the churches. I am a descendent of David, and bring tidings of rebirth (morning star—see; 2:28).

16. I Jesus have sent mine angel to testify unto you these things in the churches. I am the root and the offspring of David, and the bright and morning star.

17. "And the Lamb and his bride, say, 'Come'. And those who understand these mysteries say 'Come'. And let those who thirst for truth come; and whosoever will, let him partake of the knowledge of these things freely.

17. And the Spirit and his bride say, Come. And let him that heareth say, Come. And let him that is athirst come. And whosoever will, let him take the water of life freely.

18. "For I testify to every person to whom this prophecy has been revealed that nothing can be added to it. Those who violate the will of God (deviations of natural and cosmic law) shall reap what they have sown as it has been written:

18. For I testify unto every man that heareth the words of the prophecy of this book, If any man shall add unto these things, God shall add unto him the plagues that are written in this book:

19. "And those who cease not to walk in the path of ego and self-will shall not enter into the resurrection, but remain bound to the darkness and ignorance of mortality."

19. And if any man shall take away from the words of the book of this prophecy, God shall take away his part out of the book of life, and out of the holy city, and from the things which are written in this book.

20. He testified to these things, saying, "I come quickly. Therefore come and enter the resurrection."

20. He which testifieth these things saith, Surely I come quickly. Amen. Even so, Come, Lord Jesus.

21. May the grace of the Lord Jesus Christ be with you all.

21. The grace of our Lord Jesus Christ be with you all.

AMEN

Fear not when God sends forth his Holy Spirit to abide with you all the days of your life, for then you shall be purged and freed from all defilement. This is for your good that you might dwell with Him, and He with you forever and ever.
Jesus the Christ
The Lost Jesus Scroll
Vatican MS., Section II.P.135-3

END NOTES

INTRODUCTION

1. Gold signifies spirit, and the girdle, the binding of two natures of the soul. In ancient times the lower extremities of the physical body represented the inferior nature of a human body, because it bore the organs of human waste. The upper extremities signified that which is removed from the impurities of earth, such as the heart and brain

2. Translation of *The Lost Jesus Scroll* is available through barnesandnoble.com, amazon.com, many fine bookstores and the James A. Rock Publishing Company. It was translated from Aramaic and Hebrew by Professor Edmond S Bordeaux during his studies in the Archives of the Roman Vatican and is not considered a Gnostic writing. In 1985 an announcement of a reading of the scroll was made over Vatican radio in the presence of Mr. Mario Spinelli, a Vatican journalist, and Mr. Spinelli reported, without reservation, that this manuscript did indeed exist in the labyrinths of the archives.

CHAPTER I

1. Blood denotes sacrifice and a means by which the soul can be purged of all things (sins) which are not in harmony with God. Therefore, by descending into matter, the indwelling spark of God becomes the savior of humanity.

2. As each human being resurrects the indwelling light, the soul reaps its atonement. This includes penalties for all actions and thoughts causing separation and harm to oneself and others. This period, called the dark night of the soul, is most difficult.

3. Although the seven golden candlesticks were carefully explained in the summation at the beginning of the chapter, it might be well to mention them again. These represent the wisdom or knowledge (gold) pertaining to the seven phases of earthly evolution, or seven epochs, God's Divine Plan as revealed by Mosaic Law (Genesis 1:1-31, Genesis 2:1-3).

4. The seven forces are the same seven forces as summarized at the beginning of chapter one; Power which creates, Love which unites, Wisdom which guides, Eternal Life which reveals the immortality of all life, Creative Work which builds the universe, Peace which comes in the final phase of creation when the brotherhood of mankind has been established, and finally, Oneness with the Creator.

5. In ancient times the sun at high noon signified the resurrected Christ in all his glory.

6. To reiterate this complex scripture, seven stars signify the seven epochs of soul progression, or angels presiding over the seven forces of nature. At the same time, however, they symbolize the seven heads (seven flames) which serve over the seven churches (candlesticks). The churches, in turn, form the foundation for a new religion, in the same manner which earth serves as a foundation for heaven.

CHAPTER II

1. The Nicolaitanes were followers of Nicolus of Damascus, advocate of the Jews who pleaded for Archelaus (Son of Herod the Great) in the front of Caesar against Antipater. Following Archelaus' crime of slaying a multitude which was praying around a temple during a customary festival, there were those who claimed Archelaus should forfeit his right to become heir to the throne, and declared his act of violence to be contrary to law. Nicolus, in defense, alleged the slaughter could not be avoided and the people had been slain because they were enemies of Archelaus. It fell upon Caesar to determine the validity of the charges, for it had been agreed by Herod the Great in his death papers that Caesar should choose his successor. There were those who supported Nicolus' defense of Archelaus against Antipater and these were called Nicolaitanes. The defense of Archlaus was successful and he was granted his father's rulership for a brief time.

2. This scripture suggests that those who follow the way of the Christ will be cast into prison and have tribulation for ten days (ten periods of divine transformation), or until they become one (1-0) in God. It also signifies the separation of that which is divine from that of the carnal, as it is the lower nature which is comprised of the lesser mind, emotions, and feelings, and binds the soul to matter. Therefore, the two natures separate, and the soul, because of its action through the lesser self, must suffer atonement until it is sufficiently

218

purified to become the bride of the indwelling Christ. The marriage of the soul and Christ would then allow that which is mortal to become immortal. Neither would the soul function through the lesser mind but would possess the Christed or illumined mind, as signified by the halo often painted around some of the holy figures. This is referred to as the crown of life, or the mark of immortality.

3. Antipas was a powerful man of royal lineage who dwelled in the city of Jerusalem, and in whose care the public treasures were placed. Taken to prison, his throat was cut with a sword by a man named John the Robber, son of Dorcas. Antipas was a sympathizer with the followers of Jesus the Christ, and since there were a number of other influential people imprisoned who were also put to death by the sword at the same time, a great deal of fear sprung up among the followers, should they too be executed. Later, this same band of cutthroats, who were responsible for the slaughter tried to negotiate with Rome for the surrender of Jerusalem.

4. Balaam was a Midianite prophet who lived in the Euphrates Valley at the time of Moses. He drew many followers because of his powers and was considered the greatest of all the seers in his time. When the army of Moses approached the country of the Midianites, the ambassadors of Balah sent for Balaam to entreat him to cast curses for the destruction of the Israelites. Although Balaam received the ambassadors courteously, when he sought God's will in the matter he found that God was opposed to his intentions. Later after further entreaties from the ambassadors, he decided to go along with them after all, but in route the burro upon which he rode threw him into a wall and he was injured. While he was flogging the burro, an angel appeared and informed him that the animal had done so because it was Balaam himself who was contrary to the will of God. The prophet was then greatly afraid. However, the conflict did not cease, because it was the wish of the Midianites that the followers of Moses come to worship the gods of the Midianites and Moabites. Therefore, the followers of Balaam sent forth the daughters of the land to tempt the young Hebrew men, who eventually transgressed their own laws and fell into sedition. Moses, afraid the matter would grow worse, called the people to council and eventually sent in his army, which was victorious over the land of Midian.

5. Jezebel, the daughter of Ethbaal, King of the Zidonians, and wife of Ahab, King of Israel, became famous for her idolatries and persecutions of the prophets, and she herself worshipped Baal. She once sought the death of Elijah, who prophesied to the king, her husband, that his lands, which were suffering from drought and famine, would be saved by rain. It came to pass that Elijah's signs were so much greater than those of Jezebel's prophets that she became angry and threatened his life, forcing him into exile in the city of Beersheba. Before leaving, however, the prophet predicted Jezebel's flesh would be torn into bits and eaten by animals. Shortly thereafter, Jehu, a military leader, caused Jezebel her untimely death. Upon entering the city of Jezreel, Jehu spotted Jezebel on a tower where she was standing to accuse Jehu of killing his master, and when she refused to come down, Jehu commanded his servants to throw her from the tower. Later, he suffered some attack of conscience and ordered her body to be buried because of the nobility of her blood. He found her remains had already been consumed by dogs.

CHAPTER III

1. The Star of David: King David ben Jesse, Israel's greatest King was born October 28, 1062 BC at 1:00 A.M., 35E13 3N42, in Bethlehem, Judea, one thousand fifty-five years before Jesus the Christ. The planetary configurations at his birth fell into the pattern of an interlocked double triangle, known as a double grand trine, and formed into one star. This has since been used as a Jewish symbol. The insignia denotes mastery and signifies the spirit of the redeemer which descended into matter in the beginning, (the symbol "V"), and the redeemer's ascent or resurrection from matter in the end, (an inverted "V"). These form the two interlocking triangles known as the star, or mark of David.

2. The crown is usually symbolized in art as golden and contains seven points to indicate the completion of the seven necessary cycles of soul progression, or rulership over the corporeal world. During the transformation from human to divine, or graduation from mortal to immortal, a series of mystical experiences occur which enable the soul to better understand its purpose. The newly anointed, or elect, then becomes the wearer of this crown which unites the earthly kingdom with the Heavenly Kingdom. Although the crown is invisible to the human eye, it is easily discernible to one who wears it. It was first used as a crown of thorns to signify the crucifixion of the soul, or purification of all the impure aspects which remain untrue to the indwelling Christ. The soul must

comply with Divine Will until it becomes one with it, after which the crown becomes a halo of light denoting that the metamorphosis of divine birth is complete. Those who become recipients of the crown are well aware that they are striving for mastery over the mortal nature, and they work incessantly lest they not be found worthy to continue and their souls be required to remain bound to mortality. (See: Dark Night of the Soul - St. John of the Cross.)

3. Anointing refers to pouring oil on the body, a customary but little understood symbolic rite from antiquity. To those who crossed the boundaries of the resurrection of the dead it is understood as receiving wisdom directly from the mind of God. Among those who achieved this ascended state, were such people as Moses, Elijah, Solomon, Samuel, King David, etc. Unfortunately, the average human of modern world assumes that this cannot be achieved. This is a serious misconception, for the anointing was received by several of Christ's disciples and has certainly touched numerous others through out history.

CHAPTER IV

1. Since the early days of the Egyptian dynasties, the teachings of divine birth have been considered the most secret of the secrets and have been symbolized by fish, insects, reptiles, animals and birds. Although traditional Christianity considered other religious symbolism as pagan, there has been no greater instigator of such rites than those established by Christendom. The lion, according to the ancient Christian writings, has been used to signify first born, representing the divine, or indwelling Christ nature to be resurrected in mankind. Since it was also believed that the lion slept with its eyes open, it was looked upon as guardian of the soul. Thus the statement is made "When the lion (Christ) and the lamb (soul) lie down together (state of oneness) there will be peace on earth." The calf was also an important object of worship and said to represent the sun, as well as elements of earth. Considered the most succulent of meats, it was often used in early sacrificial rites to signify purification by fire and release of the soul from its tomb of flesh. In that the impurities in mankind must be changed into divine attributes while enmeshed in the corporeal body, human-will must surrender to Divine Will. Thus, that which is divine and imprisoned in the physical state bars the soul's entry into holy union until its purification is complete, after which a human being merges into a divine being. The eagle, in Christian tradition, symbolizes one who has been born again, a modern adaptation of the Phoenix, an immortal bird signifying messiah, or savior, born from the ashes of human-will.

CHAPTER V

1. After Judah was received by his brother Joseph in Egypt, his tribe, totaling 74,600, was given approximately one-third of the land west of the Jordan River. During Judah's march through the desert to meet with his princely brother, he carried a tribal standard, or flag. This was green in color and bore the symbol of the Lion, meaning first born. John the Beloved now used the tribal demarcation in Verse 5 to represent the Light manifestation in the beginning which brought creation into fruition. This Light is the indwelling Christ in mankind.

2. Although the term sacrifice, as it is used in this scripture, should be well understood by this time, one must remember that John the Beloved is still speaking of the indwelling Christ, or Light, which descended into matter in the beginning and made life possible. In that the Light is considered the light of consciousness and the first manifested form of God, it is referred to as the Son who sacrificed, or departed, from his heavenly abode that the known universe could be brought into existence. It is only through raising Him from the dead that the soul can be redeemed.

CHAPTER VI

1. For centuries the word "horse" has been used to symbolize the mind. This was derived from the concept that the soul uses the mind much like a vehicle to get from one place to another. Since the term originated long before motorized transportation, the horse was the common carrier. For this reason the four processes of transformation, as intimated by the four beasts, are represented by four horses in the Apocalypse.

2. Revelation 6:6 speaks of the period following the resurrection of the indwelling Christ and the soul's subsequent entry into the dark night to be purged of its iniquitous ways. During this period, the Christ metes out a measure of good for good and three measures of adversities for every evil which the soul has committed. It should be understood, however, that this is done to purify the soul, that it be made ready for the holy marriage.

3. In ancient times human beings were placed upon the altar, that the body could be burned and the soul ascend to heaven. Later the rite was performed on animals for the same reason. Today, however, to symbolize the seventh day, or seventh epoch, when God will gather himself together and restore the earth, each person enters the church of his or her choice on the Sabbath, to sit before

the altar, thereby sacrificing the earthly life for the unification of the soul and the spirit through the world of God (11:00 A.M. to 12 high noon, the designated hour of the resurrection). In this manner the holy edifice connotes a bridge between human and divine.

CHAPTER VII

1. John used the term Israel throughout the apocalyptic discourse to symbolize not only the entire nation, but also the entire world. At the time the vision came to him it followed the tradition of presenting itself to the senses through familiar symbolism. However, what is applicable to one nation is also applicable to all nations, because the natural and cosmic laws are common to every human being. Thus, the twelve tribes of Israel symbolized the elect, or those in the world who raised the indwelling Christ.

CHAPTER VIII

1. In obedience to God's command in the wilderness, Moses had his metal workers make two long silver trumpets (silver - ancient alchemical symbol for the soul). These were used to call the congregation to worship, as well as signaling the beginning of each nomadic journey of the Hebrew as they traveled from one place to another. Later, throughout the generations which ensued, the sons of Aaron, high priest over the desert wanderers, continued to use trumpets to call the Israelites to worship and remind them of deliverance from their enemies. John the Beloved uses the same symbols to indicate the purifying forces which will deliver the soul from its indiscretions.

2. There is a sub-conscious mind (sea) beyond the boundaries of corporeal senses, which separates the human nature from its divine nature. This ocean contains within it the specters of eons, the ghosts of false beliefs, and a record of past misdeeds, and it feeds the mind from its accumulated inherent tendencies. Just as human society must be cleansed of war and strife, so must the mind be cleansed of hatred and anger. The sea of accumulated desires and inherent tendencies flows through the mind, and in turn, the mind flows through the body, creating the dissension and strife which exists in the outer or human world. For this reason the battle of Armageddon must bring about the purification of the body (sense attractions of mortality), mind, and soul, if the brotherhood of man is to be realized.

3. Some clarification may be needed at this point to reiterate the fact that it is not the human body which is suffering death, but the corporeal, or mortal enticements of worldly ways. During the passage of human life the soul has committed many misdeeds, although perhaps long forgotten. Now, the tide returns and the soul will reap what it has sown, as the personal life is replaced by that which is eternal.

CHAPTER IX

1. As the soul passes through the dark night it knows that its suffering is being administered by forces it cannot see and may not even understand. However, as the days lengthen and the soul rises out of this deep abyss that it carved for itself through its defilement, the impure is destroyed, even as the good is strengthened through purgation and great revelation.

2. Although the symbolism of the Euphrates has been clarified in the chapter introduction, it is useful to further explain its usage in this scripture. According to the ancient writings the first purification is said to be that of earth. To pass this test, the body and its senses must be subdued in all its parts and become a perfect instrument of the enlightened will. The second mystery is that of water, in which the seeker of God is encompassed by a vast sea (subconscious) which separates two worlds (human and divine). He who reaches the immortal world must cross this abyss by process of purgation. The third mystery is that of fire, in which the seeker of immortality must conquer ambition, pride, and the flaming tyranny of emotional excess. The fourth mystery is air, wherein the mind develops wisdom to rise as vapor and end the corruptible reign of the senses. This never-ending flood of revelation which encompasses the soul at the time the spirit descends to live in the flesh is likened to the great river.

3. St. John of the Cross, in his "Dark Night of the Soul", describes this purgation, saying, "The first is whether, when a soul finds no pleasure consolation in the things of God, it also fails to find it in any thing created; for, as God sets the soul in this dark night to the end that He may quench and purge its sensual desire, he allows it not to find attraction or sweetness in anything whatsoever. These souls whom God is beginning to lead through these solitary places of the wilderness are like to the children of Israel, to whom in the wilderness God began to give food from Heaven, containing within itself all sweetness."

4. During this period when John wrote his "Revelation," many who did not follow the one God concept worshipped ritual and religious effigies which were presented in multitudinous forms and symbolized things adverse to the nature of God. Therefore, soliciting powers through ones belief in these false gods was prohibited and considered sorcery, although the term sorcery was not intended to include those beneficial powers bestowed upon the soul by the indwelling Christ, such as healing and prophecy.

CHAPTER X

1. Ancient Hermetic principles as outlined in Cabalistic tradition symbolize certain Hebrew customs and mysteries by diagraming the spirit of man in the form of a triangle which points downward. This lower point represents one third of the soul's nature, that part immersed in the world of matter. The remaining two-thirds, which never clothes itself in a sheath of matter, signifies the Hermetic Anthropos, the Overman of Cyclops, the guardian Daemon of the Greeks, the Angel of Jakob Boehme, and the Oversoul of Emerson. Although it is presented as an angel in Chapter X:1, it nonetheless is that divine aspect of the soul (indwelling Christ) which is not subject to the limitations of matter. Through the resurrection of the dead, the law of birth and death is transcended and the soul is consciously united with the indwelling Christ. This is the primary purpose of man.

CHAPTER XI

1. The measuring reed is described as the calamus, or sweet cane, and is used for measurement. Its length is six times a cubit, plus six handbreadths, nearly eleven feet (10'10"). It is used in Rev. 11-l to signify the pre-testing, or judgment, by the resurrected Christ (six handbreadths) to see if the soul is worthy to be raised from the corporeal world (six times a cubit).

2. As the soul enters the seventh cycle of human evolution in which the Christ must be brought forth, it has three levels of purification to undergo. These are the body, the mind, and the soul. Although the soul has passed through the initiatory phases in which it has balanced the personal versus impersonal life (fight with Lucifer), and has stood judgment by reviewing the impurities born of its association with matter, it has barely begun the arduous transformation from corporeal to divine. That which is less must yet war against that which is greater to insure all evils are dissipated.

CHAPTER XII

1. In Daniel 10:21 the archangel Michael is described as the *prince* of Israel and (12:1) as *the great prince who stands" in times of conflict over the sons of your people*. As a special guardian of the Jews, it was prophesied that Michael would defend them in their terrible time of trouble during the Great Tribulation, when the remnant would be delivered and established in the millennial kingdom. The Great Tribulation and millennial kingdom are none other than the dark night of the soul and the descent of the heavenly estate on earth referred to in the Apocalypse. John the Beloved has used the earlier prophecy here to depict Armageddon. In this case Michael represents the great regenerative force and guardian angel which defends the divinity of the soul through its struggle.

2. After the soul has given birth to the indwelling Christ and entered the wilderness of the dark night, it passes into a most remarkable state. Although it must purge the uncleanness from itself, it is also receiving great knowledge and revelations. Having already been shown the divine plan of God, which is the basis of all things, the soul is completely educated in the ways of God, including all philosophies, sciences, arts, religions, etc. During the first few years of this wondrous transformation the soul is changed from mediocrity to greatness, and becomes competent in many things. As its education has been wrought by God, it rises beyond the boundaries of academia. It is for this reason that people such as John the Beloved seem to possess great genius, although not credited with study through formal education.

3. After the spirit has descended in the flesh and soul enters the hall of judgment, where it stands final tribunal, the false ideals it has followed throughout its life of ignorance are carefully revealed. The soul, with the newly resurrected Christ, wishes to walk in the ways of God, but is unable to obliterate the past until its unlearned lessons have been learned. To escape retribution, or the disciplines required to free the soul from the chains of matter, seems impossible. The dragon (ego-self will) of this divine metamorphosis causes the soul to remember those things which have been in direct violation of natural and cosmic law until it has completed purification.

CHAPTER XIII

1. This particular anthropos denotes the most violent aspects of the three beasts which were highly revered by the people of Israel. The spots of the leopard, which is the largest carnivore (next to the bear) in the Holy land, represents the battle between the mortal and immortal natures, or darkness versus light. In comparison the bear was looked upon as cunning; its paws were powerful, and it is used here to symbolize its ferocious attack upon the soul, after the manner in which it attacks all animals which come its way. And finally, the lion represents the first born, although it attacks the soul as it attacks its animal kill. In dissecting the anthropos it should be remembered that John the Beloved used beasts and dragons to denote the lower aspects of mankind.

2. This particular anthropos depicts the afflictions wrought upon the body through misuse of natural law, which can be determined by the fact that the beast rises out of the earth. In that the action of the soul throughout its existence in matter determines the quality of the mind, the mind determines the values which are followed in the human world. Therefore, it can be said that actions in the world (beast) reflect the lower nature of the soul (ego & self-will, or dragon).

CHAPTER XIV

1. Immaculate Conception is a term which has been greatly misunderstood in religious history, for it refers to the union of the soul and God, which results in the birth of the indwelling Christ. Since this divine principle is raised in man without physical expression, or union between man and woman, such a birth is said to be holy because it is untouched by worldy enticements. For this reason many geniuses throughout history were said to have been conceived by Immaculate Conception, or divinely born.

2. Although reference is made to another angel, the usual formal order of three prevails, thereby indicating that these, and the two subsequent angels, are merely divine counterparts of the preceding dragon, and his beasts. Again these continue to symbolize certain purification taking place within the soul, mind, and body according to its good and evil.

3. When the resurrection of the dead descends upon the soul, the anguish over its iniquities is viewed as descending from God, therefore referred to in Revelation 14:19 as the wrath of God. As it is the descent of the spirit to dwell in the flesh which causes such tribulation to the soul, the symbolism is justly incorporated, although God is in reality goodness and love. He allows this purgation of the soul to prepare it for entry into the kingdom of heaven, a task which self- will could never accomplish.

CHAPTER XVI

1. Blood is defined as the fluid circulated by the heart through the vertebrate vascular system, carrying oxygen and nutrients throughout the body and waste materials to excretory channels. Therefore, the term blood has been chosen, for it reflects the good which enters the soul and which washes away its impurities. As blood is the life of the human body, Divine Will is the blood of the soul.

2. As the subconscious reveals the collective experiences of the soul, its unsavory portions are gradually transmuted into that which is good. Thus, when past adversities or subsequent misuse of natural and cosmic law in the terrestrial world no longer govern the body, mind, or soul, it is said that every living thing is dried upon the sea. St. John of the Cross in his "Dark Night of the Soul" describes this second purgation as being more difficult than the first purgation of the long dark night.

3. It is difficult to reason that a soul which has entered into the resurrection of the dead would fight against the will of God, and blame Him for the price which must be paid for every insurrection. However, the soul has long followed self-will, and finds that the state of possession by the spirit is restrictive to those endeavors which follow only the path of mortality. It is also fully aware that such divine intervention is the cause of its suffering. Therefore, it is not unnatural that the soul turns against those forces which are causing the purgation to occur.

CHAPTER XVIII

1. From the beginning of human descent into matter, the divine part of mankind, which is God, has called forth the soul to partake of the good and the beneficent. His instrument was the conscience. Unfortunately, the enticements of the corporeal world have been stronger and the soul has remained drawn to its forbidden fruit, little realizing that one day it must atone for each indiscretion, or that its dreams and desires could only be realized through the resurrection of the dead. During this age of darknes,s the soul has built up a depository of violations which descend as plagues under the precise law of cause and effect resulting from the perpetual and forward movement of God's divine plan.

2. The primary focus of attention has now turned to the material things of life, as they were known in John's time. He stresses the removal of these values because false desires have often led mankind down the road of avarice and greed, thereby causing the soul to preoccupy itself with worldly possessions. These have subsequently led to murder, rape, pillaging, selfishness, hatred, anger and war. (The color purple was included among the extravagant desires of the people because it was greatly prized, particularly Tyrian purple which was taken from the tiny mollusk found along the Phoenician coast, therefore very expensive.)

3. During the battle of Armageddon, there is always the pull between human and divine. In that the soul has dwelled in the world of matter and has become familiar with its ways, it is difficult for it to break the chains which bind it. The social world prescribes interest in family, work, and pleasure, which all too often results in severe attachments, creating jealousy, anger, and unbridled passions. It also tends to build materiality, and indulgence in those things which are harmful to the body, mind, soul, and planet. Although the soul is shown the path of good, it is still difficult to release itself from the familiarity of human life, thereby causing great torment.

CHAPTER XIX

l. There has long been an argument over which came first, sound\word or light. The East would say sound, the West would say light, although both came into being simultaneously. There can be no creation without both the light of consciousness and vibration, for God is not a deity possessing a mouth which speaks words. He is both the non-manifested and manifested aspects of over one hundred billion galaxies, and there is no place he is not. Since He manifests as both light and sound, He can best be summed up by a singular Old Testament word, LAW, or the manifestation of one will. For this reason the ancient mysteries depict the Son of God as the Light of consciousness and divine counterpart of the soul abiding in all life. The Greek word Christos (Christ), meaning anointed, would be the most applicable here, although the names Adonai, Lord, and Jehovah, Elohim, and Yahweh, have also been used in this context by various sects.

2. In biblical times, the hand was placed under the thigh to symbolize an oath derived from the relationship of the hip and the regenerative organs (Gen.46:26). In Revelation 19:16, John the Beloved uses oath according to Hebrew law, invoking the name of God, or a sworn covenant.

3. Gravitation is a law of the world of finite matter, and is the impulse toward the ways of human life. Levitation, on the other hand, is a law of the spiritual world and creates an impulse toward spiritual things. Since a bird is capable of neutralizing gravity it is considered to partake of a nature superior to other terrestrial creations, therefore a symbol of divinity. Thus angels have been illustrated with wings like birds, because they represent a soul which has transcended worldly attachments to inhabit a middle kingdom between God and human. For this reason, John used birds in Revelation 19:17 to illustrate messengers of God who would destroy, or eat, the remaining impure aspects of the corporeal nature during the last and final battle.

CHAPTER XX

1. In the beginning, when the indwelling Christ descended into matter and brought the soul into consciousness, he was limited by the influence of the soul's corporeal senses and attraction to matter. Because the soul served as intermediary between heaven and matter, that part of it enmeshed in matter became less, or a lower nature (Satan). Through the resurrection of the indwelling Christ the soul puts away its false values and seeks unity with its divine

counterpart. During this first part of the courtship all is well. However, the temptations buried in the subconscious still must be further purified. Therefore, the indwelling Christ causes the soul to work through this lesser nature to transmute and change it in preparation for final union. In the Via Delorosa this phase of divine metamorphosis is known as the final phase of the resurrection, when the stone (the final throes of the ego) is rolled away from the tomb.

2. The first death refers to the descent of the indwelling Christ into matter, which bound him to mortality along with the soul. This assured redemption to the soul, as it evolved through the seven progressive epochs of necessity (said to have died for the sins of humankind). When the indwelling Christ is raised, the process is reversed, for he and his bride, the soul, exchange mortality for immortality, therefore dying to the personal life which was once governed by human-will (second death).

3. It is well to reiterate that the holy city is not a specific location, either on the earth, or in the vast universe of the stars. Rather it is a state of consciousness which will possess mankind's future world, for it exists in all humans. It is the state which has been achieved by every saint and seeker who has surrendered ego and self-will. Perhaps this is one of the greatest promises of the Apocalypse; that any human being can dwell in heaven, as well as on earth and beyond.

CHAPTER XXI

1. Most of Revelation 21:12 is outlined in the chapter introduction. However, there is one other codicil which might further clarify John the Beloved's reference to the names of the twelve tribes of Israel. As he perceived the future state of the city of Jerusalem, he saw that the old dispensation would pass away through the restoration of original teachings of Moses. In other words, as the people entered divine metamorphosis, a new nation would rise from the ashes of the old. This would encompass the twelve tribes which descended from the twelve sons of Jacob.

2. The interpretation of Revelation 21:14 is the same as that which was outlined in Odyssey 21:12 with one exception. In that the Hebrew nation was originally established by the twelve sons of Jacob, the new Israel would be brought forth through the teachings of the twelve apostles of Jesus the Christ.

BIBLIOGRAPHY

Apocrypha. Cambridge at University Press, Great Britain.

The Apocryphal New Testament. Translated by Dr. Montague Rhode James, Litt. D., F.B.A., F.S.A. Provost of Eton, Oxford University Press, London, England, 1926.

The Apocryphal New Testament. William Wake, M.R., D.D., Archbishop of Canterbury, and Rev. Nathaniel Lardner, D.D., published by Simkin Marshall, Hamilton, Kent and Co., Glasgow, Scotland.

The Apocryphal New Testament. Simpkin, Marshall, Hamilton, Kent and Co., London, England.

The Archko Volume or *The Archeological Writings of the Sanhedrin and Talmud of the Jews.* Translated by Drs. McIntosh and Twyman, Keats Publishing, Inc., New Canaan, Connecticut. 1975.

Augustine. Robert Meagher, New York University, 1978

Augustine of Hippo. Peter Brown, University of California Press, 1978

The Babylonian Genesis. Alexander Heidel, University of Chicago Press, Chicago and London, 1942

The Bible as History. Werner Keller, 1909, Translated from German by William Neil. Published by William Morrow and Co., Inc., N.Y.

The Book of Enoch. R.H. Charles, D. Litt., D.D., Clarendon Press, 1964

Complete Works - The Second Birth. Omraam Mikhael Aivanhov Prosveta, U.S.A. edition.

The Day Christ Died. Jim Bishop, Harper and Row, San Francisco.

The Dead Sea Scrolls. Edmund Wilson, Oxford University Press, 1969.

The Dead Sea Scrolls and the Bible. Charles F. Pfeiffer, Baker Book House Co., 1969.

The Dead Sea Scrolls and the Christian Myth. John M. Allegro, Westbridge Books, 1979.

DeSanto Joseph at Arimathea. Emperor Heodusia (found in Pilate's Praelorium in Jerusalem - AD 379)

The Drama of the Last Disciples. George F. Jowett, Published by Covenant Publishing Co., Ltd., London, England, 1975.

Eusebius, History of the Church from Christ to Constantine. Translated by G.A. Williamson, Penguin, 1965.

Gods, Graves and Scholars, The History of Archaeology. C.C. Ceram. Bantam Books, 1967.

The Galilean - A Life of Christ. Albert DePina, House-Warven Publishers, Hollywood, California, 1951.

The Gospel According to Thomas. Coptic Text, translated by A. Guillaumont and Yassah Abd Al Masih, Harper and Row, New York, 1959.

Harper Bible Dictionary. Madeline S. Miller and J. Lane Miller, Harper and Row, New York, 1973.

The Hebraic Tongue Restored. Fabre d'Olivet, Samuel Weiser, Inc., York Beach, Maine, 1976

Hermes and Plato. Edouard Schure - translated by F. Rothwell, B.A., William Rider and Son, Ltd., London, England, 1972

History of the Britons. Nennius, England, 796.

History of the First Council of Nice. Dean Dudley, Attorney at Law, Copyright A.D. 1886, published by Peter Echler Publishing Co., 1925.

The Holy Bible from Ancient Eastern Manuscripts. Translated from the Peshitta by George M. Lamsa, 1933, Published by A.J. Holman Company, Nashville, Tennessee.

The Holy Bible. Translated out of original tongues by His Majesty's King James special command. Printed by His Majesty's Printer, Eyre and Spottiswoode, Ltd., London, England.

The Holy Kabbalah. by A.E. Waite, University Books, Citadel Press.

An Introduction to the Cabala - Tree of Life. Z'ev ben Shimon Halevi, Samuel Weiser, Inc., New York, 1972.

Israel and the Dead Sea Scrolls. Edmond Wilson, Farrar, Straus and Giroux, New York, 1978.

The Israelites. Time Life Books, catalogue card no. 75-4101.

Jerusalem History Atlas. Martin Gilbert, MacMillan Publishing Co., New York.

Jesus. Michael Grant, Weidenfeld and Nicholson, London.

Joseph of Arimathea. Skeats, University Press, 1871.

Josephus Complete Works. The Antiquities of the Jews and the War of the Jews. Translated by William Whiston, A.M. 1867. Published by Porter and Coates, Philadelphia, Pennsylvania. Republished in 1963 by Kregel Publications, Grand Rapids, Michigan.

The Koran. Translated by N.J. Dawood, Penguin Books, 1963.

The Letters of the Younger Pliny. Translated by Betty Radiel, Penguin Books, 1963.

Life in Ancient Egypt. Adolph Erman, translated by H.M. Terard, Dover Publications, Inc., New York.

Life of St. Mary Magdelene. Maurus Rabanus, Archbishop of Meyenie, England.

Lives of the Saints. Translated by J.F. Webb, Penguin Books, 1965.

The Lost Years of Jesus Revealed. Rev. Dr. Charles Francis Potter, Fawcett Publications, Inc., 1962.

Magna Tabula Glastoniae. Pynson (currently in possession of the House of Howard) England.

Metrical Life of St. Joseph. Pynson, England, 1520.

Morals and Dogma of the Ancient and Accepted Scottish Rite of Freemasonry. Prepared for the council of the Thirty-third Degree. Entered into the Library of Congress at Washington, D.C., 1871, published by L.H. Jenkins, Inc., Richmond, Virginia.

The Mystical Doctrine of St. John of the Cross. Selected by R.H.J. Stewart, Sheed and Ward, London.

Nag Hammadi Library. Translated by members of the Coptic Gnostic Library Project of the Institute for Antiquity and Christianity, Harper and Row Publishers, New York, 1977.

New Testament Apocrypha. Edited by Professor Wilhelm Schneemelcher, University of Bonn. English translation edited by R. Wilson, Ph.D. Theol., Westmister Press, Philadelphia, Pennsylvania.

The Odes of Solomon: Original Christianity Revealed. Robert Winterhalter, Llewellyn Publications, St. Paul, Minnesota, 1985.

Old Testament Light. George M. Lamsa, Harper and Row, 1893.

The Orthodox Church. Timothy Ware, Penguin Books, 1963.

The Oxford Dictionary of Saints. David Hugh Farmer, Oxford University Press, 1978.

Pagan and Christian Creeds: Their Origin and Meaning. Edward Carpenter, Harcourt Brace and Co., New York.

Philo of Alexandria. Samuel Sandmel, Oxford University Press, New York, 1979

Pistis Sophia. Extracts from the *Book of the Savior* and excerpts from a cognate literature by G.H.S. Mead, M.A., published by John M. Watkins, London, England.

Primitive Christianity - Vol. I, II, III, and IV. Otto Pfleiderer, D.D., Reference Book Publishers, Inc., New Jersey, 1965.

Saints—Their Cults and Origins. Caroline Williams, St. Martin's Press, New York, 1980.

Shroud. Robert K. Wilson, Bantam Books, 1977.

The Shroud of Turin. Ian Wilson, Doubleday and Co., Inc., New York, 1979.

Southern Palestine and Jerusalem. W.M. Thomson, Harper and Brothers, 1982.

St. Francis of Assisi. Morris Bishop, Little Brown and Co., Boston, 1974.

St. Joseph of Arimathea at Glastonbury. Kiovel Smithett Lewis, late Vicar of Glastonbury, published by James Clarke and Co., Cambridge, England, 1922.

Unger's Bible Dictionary. Merrill F. Unger, 1957-1980, Moody Press, Chicago, Illinois.

The Westminster Dictionary of the Bible. John D. Davis, Ph.D., D.D., Westminster Press, Philadephia, 1944.

Wild Branch on the Olive Tree. Father William Treacy and Rabbi Raphael Levine in collaboration with Sister Patricia Jacobsen, Binford and Mort Publishers.

The Wycliffe Bible Commentary. Edited by Charles F. Pfeifer - Old Testament, and Everett F. Harrison, New Testament, Moody Press, Chicago, Illinois, 1962

INDEX

Christ, Jesus and the Essenes
  as messiah, 131
  as savior, 42
  followers of, 18, 219
  revelation of, 8
  secret teachings of,
  testimony of, 8, 10, 119, 182
Christ Consciousness (Soul
  Consciousness), xi
Christed (illumined) mind, 28, 29,
  134, 188, 219
Christian (s), 39, 81, 222
  early, 17
  literature, 99
  mysteries, 65, 81, 91, 142, 147
  mystics, xviii
Christianity, xix
  ancient writings of, 196, 222
  philosophy, 100, 112
  scriptures, 16, 29, 31, 99
  secret teachings of, xii
Christos, 182, 183, 230
chrysalis, 81
chrysolyte, 199, 207
chrysoprasus, 200, 207
Clemens, Bishop of Rome, xii
  Apostolic Constitution, xii
Clemons, Bishop of Alexandria, xiii
  Stromata, xiii
clouds, 5, 10, 92
communions , xvii
  with angels, xviii
  with Sons of Heaven, 45
copper, 6
cosmic law, xvii 6, 9, 13, 15, 16, 18,
  27, 38, 41, 46, 49, 65, 74, 75,
  77, 78, 119, 141, 142, 143,
  214, 223, 227, 228

crown(s)
  of gold, 41
  of life, 16, 20, 219
  of thorns, 221
  of twelve stars, 115
crystal
  glass sea like, 42
  clear as, 204, 211, 221
crucifixion of the soul, xii, 75, 91
  See also resurrection of the dead
Cyril of Alexandria, St., 111, 112
David ben Jesse, 221
Dead (not awakened), xviii
Dead Sea Scrolls, 25, 114, 233, 234
Dead Sea Scriptures, 45, 52
  Hymn of the Initiates, 45
Death, xviii
  first death, 16, 189, 231
  second death, 16, 20, 187, 189,
    192, 194, 203, 231
Degrees of sacrament, xii
descent
  of New Israel, xv, xix
  indwelling Christ, 8, 12, 35, 49,
    68, 103, 231
  New Jerusalem, 7, 32, 38, 112,
    141, 160, 177, 196, 204, 226
  soul's descent into matter, 49, 90,
    229
  spirit to live in the flesh, 7, 32,
    112, 141, 160, 177, 196, 204,
    226
devil, See also dragon, satan, serpent,
    204, 231
  lower nature, 16, 118, 188
Dionysius, St. Bishop of Athens, xii

five months, 82, 87, 88

Flavius, Josephus, Antiquities of the Jews, 198

foundation (s), xix, xx, xxi
  of world, 29, 126
  twelve layers of in the Holy City, 38, 200

four
  angels, 63, 64, 67, 89
  beasts, 48, 51, 54, 58, 59, 63, 70, 134, 144, 178, 180, 198, 207, 223
  cardinal points, 63, 64, 67, 84
  corners of earth, 67
  elements, xxi
  foundations, 89
  four and twenty elders, 41, 43, 49, 51, 107, 180
  horns, 83, 88, 237
  horses, 45, 53, 64, 197, 201, 223
  seasons, 63
  weeks, 84
  winds, 63, 67

foursquare, 198, 206

fourteen angels (according to Moses), xviii

Francis of Assisi, St., xviii, 236

Garden of Eden, 121, 122

Gideon over the Midianites, 150

Gog and Magog, 189, 193

gold, xvi, xvii
  altar, 242
  candlesticks, xvi, 6
  girdle, xvi, xvii, 6, 11, 217
  reed to measure, 205
  streets of New Jerusalem, 102, 160, 200
  vials, 46, 47, 49, 144

Gospel
  Of John, xx
  of Peace, 239
  of Thomas, 3, 234

Harp (s), 46, 47, 49, 134

half time (hour, day), 74, 84

harlot, 157 , 159, 167, 168

Heavenly Father, xviii, 25
  See also Father, 9, 15, 24, 25, 30, 33, 35, 97, 99, 102

Hebraic Tongue Restored, xiv, 122, 234

Hebrew, xiv, xv
  Balal, 157, 238, 242
  breastplate, 38, 65, 198, 199
  breastplates of fire, 84, 89
  breastplates of iron, 83, 87
  Har Megiddo, 150, 154
  mysteries, 46, 99, 198, 211, 238
  symbolism, 83, 88

Hermes, 97, 237

high noon, 74, 77, 84, 105, 118, 218, 223, 248

Holy Bible, 234
  King James, xiv

holy bridegroom, 148, 176

Holy City, 38, 103, 160, 187, 193, 196, 197, 198, 200, 202, 208, 214, 231

holy marriage
  holy wedding, holy union, 153. 223, 240
  marriage of soul to indwelling Christ, 116, 132, 148
  to the lamb, 138

holy, xi, xvii, xviii, xix, xxi
  of the Holies, 88

Mysteries, xii, xiii, xvi, xvii, xviii,
xix, xxii, 28, 50, 54, 100, 111,
126, 129, 132, 214, 230
apocalyptic, 6, 158
Arc of the Covenant, 237
Christ, 65, 81, 142, 147, 196,
239
Elusian, xii
first born, 183
harp, 46
mind, 102
Mosiac, xv, 65, 196, 225
mother of the Mysteries, 112
transformation, 56, 203
resurrection, 8, 10, 17, 19, 23,
27, 135
natural law, xxii
Nazianzen, St. Gregory, Bishop of
Constantinople, xiii
Nebuchadnezzer II,157
Nephthalim, tribe of, 68, 199
new heaven and earth, 196, 202
New
Israel, xv, xix, 23
Jerusalem, 7, 32, 38, 65, 112,
122, 141, 148, 160, 177, 188,
196, 197, 198, 200, 202
Nicolas defends Archelaus, 16
Nicolaitanes, doctrines of, 19, 21,
218
north (death and winter), 63, 197,
205
number of man, 123, 129
oil and wine, 55
Olivet, Fabre d, xiv
oneness, 160, 218
with God, 32, 34, 84, 106, 113,
132, 182, 187, 205

with indwelling Christ, xxi 91,
191, 196, 222
Ostiarii, xii
palm branches, 66
Passover, (from human to divine),
35, 81, 181
Patmos, Isle of, xx, 4, 8, 10, 92, 187
pearls, 162, 173, 174, 200, 207
perdition, 59, 159, 163, 164
Pergamos, church of, 11, 16, 20
Philadelphia, church of, 11, 28, 31
Philosopher's stone, 17
Phoenix, 222
Pillars, 29
of fire, 92, 94
plagues, 104, 141, 142, 143, 150,
152, 170, 172, 204, 214, 229,
238
atonement, 83, 90, 94, 144, 170,
245
seven, 144, 145, 204, 238
possession, state of, 81, 229
Prince of Peace, 177
Purgation, *See also* purification, 168,
203, 225, 229
and purification, 147, 152, 158,
178, 185, 224, 228
Purification, xii
breastplates of, 83, 84, 87, 89,
238
by air, 7, 63, 64, 67, 84, 86, 101,
154, 225
by fire, 222
by water, 63, 135, 151, 153, 203,
210, 211, 214, 225
degree of sacrament, 240
of soul, xvii

244

www.ingramcontent.com/pod-product-compliance
Lightning Source LLC
Chambersburg PA
CBHW031946090426
42739CB00006B/109